To

Date

FAMILY
CHRISTIAN
PRESS

ABOVE ALL ELSE
Directions for life

WOMEN

Above all else, guard your heart, for it affects everything you do.
Proverbs 4:23-27 NLT

The quoted ideas expressed in this book (but not scripture verses) are not, in all cases, exact quotations, as some have been edited for clarity and brevity. In all cases, the author has attempted to maintain the speaker's original intent. In some cases, quoted material for this book was obtained from secondary sources, primarily print media. While every effort was made to ensure the accuracy of these sources, the accuracy cannot be guaranteed. For additions, deletions, corrections or clarifications in future editions of this text, please write FAMILY CHRISTIAN PRESS.

Scripture quotations are taken from:

The Holy Bible, King James Version

The Holy Bible, New International Version (NIV) Copyright © 1973, 1978, 1984, by International Bible Society. Used by permission of Zondervan Publishing House. All rights reserved.

The New American Standard Bible®, (NASB) Copyright © 1960, 1962, 1963, 1968, 1971, 1972, 1973, 1975, 1977, 1995 by The Lockman Foundation. Used by permission.

The Holy Bible, New King James Version (NKJV) Copyright © 1982 by Thomas Nelson, Inc. Used by permission.

The Holy Bible, New Living Translation, (NLT) Copyright © 1996. Used by permission of Tyndale House Publishers, Inc., Wheaton, Illinois 60189. All rights reserved.

New Century Version®. (NCV) Copyright © 1987, 1988, 1991 by Word Publishing, a division of Thomas Nelson, Inc. All rights reserved. Used by permission.

The Holy Bible: Revised Standard Version (RSV). Copyright 1946, 1952, 1959, 1973 by the Division of Christian Education of the National Council of the Churches of Christ in the United States of America. All rights reserved. Used by permission.

The Holy Bible, The Living Bible (TLB), Copyright © 1971 owned by assignment by Illinois Regional Bank N.A. (as trustee). Used by permission of Tyndale House Publishers, Inc., Wheaton, Illinois 60189. All rights reserved.

The Message (MSG) This edition issued by contractual arrangement with NavPress, a division of The Navigators, U.S.A. Originally published by NavPress in English as THE MESSAGE: The Bible in Contemporary Language copyright 2002-2003 by Eugene Peterson. All rights reserved.

The Holman Christian Standard Bible™ (HOLMAN CSB) Copyright © 1999, 2000, 2001 by Holman Bible Publishers. Used by permission.

Cover Design by Kim Russell / Wahoo Designs
Page Layout by Bart Dawson

ISBN 1-58334-370-9

ABOVE ALL ELSE
Directions for life

WOMEN

Above all else, guard your heart, for it affects everything you do.

Proverbs 4:23-27 NLT

TABLE OF CONTENTS

Above all else, guard your heart, for it affects everything you do. Avoid all perverse talk; stay far from corrupt speech. Look straight ahead, and fix your eyes on what lies before you. Mark out a straight path for your feet; then stick to the path and stay safe. Don't get sidetracked; keep your feet from following evil.

Proverbs 4:23-27 NLT

ABOVE ALL ELSE . . .

A PARABLE BY TIM WAY

To the casual observer, the old man might have appeared to be dead. He had sat slumped in the large chair for the past three hours—his chin resting on his chest, eyes closed. Every now and then, his eyelids would twitch, or a soft sigh would escape his throat, but other than that, he was perfectly still. An undignified stream of drool had slowly rolled from one corner of his mouth and run into his white beard.

King Solomon was asleep.

The harsh sound of pottery smashing against a wall suddenly interrupted his peace. It was not close, mind you, but close enough to filter into his subconscious and bring him into that foggy place between sleep and wakefulness. For several minutes, he drifted back and forth.

When he'd earlier let weariness overtake him, it was just after noon. Now through half-closed eyelids, he could see that the late afternoon sun pierced through the western windows of the large study at a sharp angle, sending shafts of light through the latticework in the two narrow openings. The brightness made bold geometric patterns on the floor. He sat for some time contemplating the flecks of dust floating in the hazy glow, watching the patterns of light in their almost imperceptible march across the room.

He raised his head. "I love this place," he thought as he looked around. Of all the private rooms in his palace, this study was his favorite—a place he visited often. Now in the later part of his reign, he came here almost daily. Some days he came to escape the grueling pace of palace life, some days to write, and some days just to think or take a nap. Most would consider this sitting and watching and thinking a waste of time, but he did not. Sitting, watching, and thinking had been the genesis of numerous revelations.

"What woke me?" he muttered. "No, not you," he said as he looked down at the large, sleeping dog whose gray muzzle rested on his feet. No one else in his kingdom dared assume such an intimate closeness. "You're almost as ancient as me, old girl," the old king chuckled as he reached to scratch the dog's shaggy head.

Then he heard it again—crashing pottery followed by angry voices coming from the women's chambers. He moaned. "Not again. Why can't they get along? I should have stopped with only one. What made me think that seven hundred wives could exist peacefully with each other? They are like the constant dripping of water, wearing me down little by little. And there are hundreds of them, always nagging, whining, shouting and yapping like a bunch of spoiled children from sunup to sundown."

He put his head in his hands and sighed deeply.

While he only kept fifty or so of his most favored wives at the main palace, even that was no guarantee that they would not become violent with each other. Some did not even speak his language, and some he had only seen on their wedding day. Most of them he had married as a part of what he considered the cost of keeping peace with his neighbors. "And they are quite a cost," he thought. "They have cost me peace of mind and a part of my soul." He was so much closer to Yahweh before all of this marrying and accumulation of wealth.

The king's study was a perfect square—the top story of a tower sitting in the middle of the palace wall, extending four stories up from the ground. The tower's western wall formed a part of the outer wall of the palace. There were windows on all sides—two on each wall. The eastern windows overlooked a large courtyard in the interior of the palace. The courtyard, over three hundred square feet, was surrounded on three sides by the palace's interior buildings, and on the west by the outer wall and the tower. The western windows looked out over one of the busiest streets in Jerusalem. Here, people moved about in their daily routines, unaware that they were often being observed by the king. The north and south windows of the tower room looked down each length of the western palace wall. To the south, he could see the walls of the great temple with the Holy Place extending toward the heavens. The walls of the Holy Place were trimmed in pure gold and gleamed in the setting spring sun. Of all his accomplishments, the Temple of Yahweh was his most prized.

Two of his soldiers could be seen moving along the palace wall on patrol. They were dressed in the crisp blue and white dress uniform of the palace guard. Each carried a polished bronze shield that was a replica of the pure gold shields hanging in the great ceremonial hall, and their spears were tipped with genuine silver. His soldiers were not there because of any known threats to the kingdom, but because prudence demanded that they remain on guard. Besides, the palace walls were three stories high and the entire complex stood as a virtual fortress in the middle of one of the most fortified cities in the world.

The study's stone walls were lined with fragrant cedar from Lebanon. Even though the paneling had been installed fifteen years prior, it still had a sweet fragrance that greeted visitors to the room. Tapestries of incomparable value hung over the paneling—gifts from kings in surrounding countries. The furniture was heavy and finely carved, most of it built for appearance rather than comfort. But the chair in which the king sat was designed specifically for his rather stout frame. Its perfect fit and thick padding, along with a built-in footrest made this the perfect place for thinking—and sleeping.

The room was not originally intended to be a private

study. It was actually built as a part of the defensive aspects of the palace, but because of the extended peace, it was not needed for that purpose. So, the king had long ago claimed it as his personal study—a private sanctuary and his place to write letters, proverbs and poetry. The perfect view of the city and the temple, and the solitude it provided, made this simple room the king's most favorite spot on earth.

Solomon sat for another twenty minutes watching the sun's slow march across the stone floor. It was approaching twilight. Reaching for the wine goblet, he snorted in frustration when he found it empty. He was about to ring the bell to summon a servant when he heard voices filtering up from the street below.

"Here they are again," he said to the dog. Grunting loudly, he pulled himself up out of the chair and shuffled across to the window, the dog following closely but lazily at his heels.

Looking down through the ornate lattice work to the street below, he watched a group of young men in their late teens standing together. They were noisy and brash with a cockiness that came from inexperience and youth. Their voices were far too loud, and even though it was early evening, they were well on their way to being drunk. Their bragging about yet unaccomplished exploits only enhanced their foolishness. If they were trying to impress the palace guards looking down from the wall, they were wasting their time. Real men like his soldiers were only mildly amused by boys pretending to be men.

He had observed them here before. They frequented a tavern two streets over, and were just beginning to discover the joys of wasting their fathers' money on wine and who knows what all else.

The king shook his head. "If only they realized how utterly foolish they sound!" He was glad that his son, Rehoboam, was not a part of this group. "But only because I won't let him. If I gave him half a chance he would be down there with them. No, on second thought, he would be down there leading them in their folly," he thought.

The group began to move up the street to his right. One young man, however, hung back. "Hey, Judah, are you coming with us?" they called out to him.

"Uh, no. Not right now. You go on ahead. Maybe I'll catch up later. The usual place?" Judah replied, glancing over his shoulder as he spoke.

"Okay. Sure. Your loss!" they shouted back as they walked away.

"Maybe there is hope for this one," the old king thought. But then he looked up the street to his left and saw her. She was slowly pacing back and forth at the head of the lane. He had seen her before. She was in her late twenties; the only wife of an old wealthy merchant who often left Jerusalem to travel to Lebanon and beyond in search of wares to sell in his shop. She had married him not for love, but for his money. Now, as she often did when left by herself, she had painted her face and had traded her everyday clothes for a costume more suited to her true nature. Her clothes were clearly intended to attract the men that visited this street in search for a companion for the night—for a price. Here, on the other side of the city from her home, she could pretend to be someone else, luring men into a squalid rented room that she paid for from the profits of her part-time trade.

What motivated her to act like a prostitute? Was it the money? Not likely. Her husband gave her anything she wanted. Was it the excitement or the need to feel desired? No one aside from her and Yahweh would ever know.

The young man had seen this woman standing on this corner before and had determined that he would one day work up enough courage to approach her. For a price, he knew that he could have her for the evening, even though under normal circumstances, she would not give his young face a second glance.

She stood with her hands on her hips, watching him approach. His steps were a little unsteady, betraying his inability to handle his wine. He was trying his best to act nonchalant, but was unsuccessful in the attempt. Glancing nervously this way and that, he was obviously trying to assure that his father or one of his father's associates was not watching. When he was about five feet away from her, she shocked him by running up, boldly taking his face in her hands, and kissing him full on the mouth.

"Stop!" the king cried out. "You fool!" For a moment Judah hesitated. What was that he had just heard? He looked nervously behind him. Seeing no one, he gave his attention back to the woman.

She threw her head back and laughed loudly. "Come with me, my love. I have the makings of a feast—today I made my offerings, my vows are all paid!" The sound of her voice carried from the street up to the tower window.

"This woman is fit only for stoning," the king muttered to himself. "Moses and my father David would not have put up with this foolishness. Why have we gone so far astray from the ancient ways? The very nerve this woman has—to bring the things of God into this sinful act!"

The young man looked frantically around him. He had not expected her to be so bold or so loud. He was beginning to regret his decision. Besides, she did not look as good up close as she did from the other end of the street, and her breath smelled of stale wine.

"So now I've come to find you, hoping to catch sight of your face—and here you are!" she continued loudly.

"You liar!" thought the king. "You would have latched onto the first idiot that came down the street with money in his pocket."

Putting her arms around the young man and pulling him close, she purred, "Come, my love. I've spread fresh, clean sheets on my bed, colorful imported linens. My bed is covered with spices and exotic fragrances. Come! Let's make love all night and spend the night in ecstatic lovemaking! My husband's not home. He's away on business and he won't be back for a month."

With that, she put her arm through the young man's, and steered him down the street like a sheep going to slaughter, laughing loudly as she led him out of sight.

"If her husband finds out who has been sleeping with her while he is gone, he will have one of his servants cut out this young fool's heart and throw it to his dogs," the king thought. He was suddenly overcome with a great sadness—for the young man and for all of the young men in his nation. "Why, oh why, my Lord, do they behave so foolishly? Why do they act in this manner?"

While he hadn't actually expected an answer, one came clearly and immediately. The sudden impact almost drove him to his knees.

"It is because they have such poor example as a king," the Spirit spoke. "It is because the spiritual fervor has left your kingdom and has been replaced by a shallow, token nod to me, Yahweh, in the midst of obscene materialism. I have blessed you, but you have squandered my blessings by forgetting me!"

Solomon slowly sank into the chair at the desk. Holding his head in his hands, he slowly rocked back and forth as he let the words from the Spirit sink deep into his soul. His mind drifted back over the years of his reign. What promise! What blessings! Now, nothing was left but regrets and broken potential. He had more wealth than he could count, yet he was miserable. His people were wandering further and further away from Yahweh. How could so much be right, and yet everything be so wrong? Oh, for the smile of Yahweh once again!

Solomon sighed as he picked up the quill lying on the desk and dipped it in the inkwell. It had been a long time since he had felt the Spirit stirring in him. Years of self indulgence had dulled the moving of Yahweh on his soul, and the occurrences of divine inspiration on his writing had all but stopped. Today, however, was different. The Spirit's moving had started long before dawn and had continued into the noon hour. The words seemed to spill out of him onto the parchment. It was like years ago, when he regularly felt Yahweh's tug on his heart.

He looked at the last words he had written in the hours before his nap. His thoughts were of his son, Rehoboam, the one that would likely inherit the kingdom. "The boy is brash and foolish," he thought. "He speaks without thinking. Without my strong hand on his backside he would be out on the street with those other drunken fools. He listens to no one but the young men that surround him—young pups of privilege who are totally out of touch with the people. How will he govern a people he does not even understand or care about? Oh, if only he were more like his grandfather, David. I fear for the people of Israel when I go to be with my fathers."

Early that morning, Solomon had walked up the flight of stairs to the tower room and sat in this very spot watching the sun rise over the palace buildings. The Spirit had stirred deeply on his soul and he had written, *"The path of the righteous is like the first gleam of dawn, shining ever brighter till the full light of day. But the way of the wicked is like deep darkness; they do not know what makes them stumble."*

His thoughts went back to the young man on the street. "This could apply fully to him," the king thought. "He is stumbling around in the dark and will end up in a hole that will destroy him."

His thoughts went to his own son. As he began to write, he could feel the stirring once again of the Spirit and his pen moved urgently across the parchment.

"My son, pay attention to what I say; listen closely to my words. Do not let them out of your sight, keep them within your heart; for they are life to those who find them and health to a man's whole body."

Where had he gone wrong? What were the early signs that he was going the wrong direction? His heart had once burned hot for Jehovah. He thought back to the dedication of the temple and that awesome time when the presence of God filled the Holy of Holies on that dedication day. What an experience!

Then there was God's promise to bless him when he chose wisdom over riches. And the blessings that had poured in on him were more than he could have ever imagined in his wildest dreams. He had riches, power, wisdom—success at every turn.

But something happened. Maybe it was the great success. Maybe it was the ease with which wealth came his way. Maybe it was the many wives. He could justify them by saying they were necessary to make alliances, but the fact was that Jehovah had said not to take many wives. The end result was that his heart had grown cold—almost dead.

So, he threw himself into every pursuit he could imagine; intellectual pursuits, money, power, science, and building projects. None of them brought any satisfaction. All of it was pure vanity.

He turned his eyes back to the parchment in front of him. The Spirit's warmth washed over his body, and almost as if his hand took on a life of its own, he wrote again.

"Above all else, guard your heart, for it is the wellspring of life."

"That's it!" he almost shouted. "I have let down my guard and deceived my heart."

"What should I have done, my Lord?" he whispered. The Spirit whispered back the answer softly through his soul. Tears began to course down his wrinkled face, as his quill touched the paper once again.

"Put away perversity from your mouth; keep corrupt talk far from your lips. Let your eyes look straight ahead, fix your gaze directly before you. Make level paths for your feet and take only ways that are firm. Do not swerve to the right or the left; keep your foot from evil."

Through his tears, the old king looked at what he had just written. "My God, I repent before you," he said as he fell to his old knees and wept. "I will take a spotless lamb to your temple when the sun rises in the morning, and make a proper sacrifice for my sins. Forgive me, Yahweh, for letting down the guard on my heart, for speaking in ways that displease you, for looking and coveting what was not really mine to own, and most of all, for taking paths that were not firm. It is too late for me. I have been a poor example to my sons and my nation. I fear the price they will pay for my sins. Be gracious to them, my God."

The sun had set and darkness had settled over the palace when the old king finally rose slowly and stiffly to his feet. He rang the bell for his servant. He would have something sent up from the kitchen to eat. Something simple.

Even though nothing had really changed, he suddenly felt lighter. Though the urging of the Spirit had lifted, he knew that he had probably just written the most important words of his life. He would give them to his son. Would he listen? Probably not, but he would try anyway.

If not Rehoboam, then perhaps someone else in the future would benefit from the words given to him that day by Jehovah.

My son, pay attention to what I say; listen closely to my
words.
Do not let them out of your sight, keep them within your heart;
For they are life to those who find them
And health to a man's whole body.
Above all else, guard your heart, for it is the wellspring of life.
Put away perversity from your mouth; keep corrupt talk far
from your lips.
Let your eyes look straight ahead, fix your gaze directly before
you.
Make level paths for your feet and take only ways that are
firm.
Do not swerve to the right or the left; keep your foot from evil.

Proverbs 4:20–27

While the scene of the young man and the prostitute is fictional, it has basis in fact and can be found in Proverbs 7:6–23.

INTRODUCTION

God's Word is clear: we are to guard our hearts "above all else," yet we live in world that encourages us to do otherwise. Here in the 21st century, temptations and distractions are woven into the fabric of everyday life. As believers, we must remain vigilant. Not only must we resist Satan when he confronts us, but we must also avoid those places where Satan can most easily tempt us. And, this book is intended to help.

In Proverbs 4:23-27, we are instructed to guard our words, our eyes, and our path. This text examines these instructions through a collection of essays, Bible verses, and quotations from noted Christian women.

As a way of introducing these ideas, this book begins with a parable by Tim Way—a story about temptation in the ancient city of Jerusalem and about how human waywardness, coupled with divine insight, might have influenced the writings of an aged king. Tim's story is followed by a series of practical lessons, lessons about protecting ourselves against the trials and temptations that have become inescapable elements of modern-day life.

Each day, you must make countless choices that can bring you closer to God, or not. When you guard your heart—and when you live in accordance with God's commandments—you will inevitably earn His blessings. But if you make unwise choices, or if you yield to the temptations of this difficult age, you must pay a price for your shortsightedness, perhaps a very high price.

Would you like to avoid the dangers and temptations that Satan will inevitably place along your path? And would you like to experience God's peace and His abundance? Then guard your heart above all else. When you're tempted to speak an unkind word, hold your tongue. When you're faced with a difficult choice or a powerful temptation, seek God's counsel and trust the counsel He gives. When you're uncertain of your next step, follow in the footsteps of God's only begotten Son. Invite God into your heart and live according to His commandments. When you do, you will be blessed today, tomorrow, and forever.

PART 1

GUARD
YOUR WORDS

*Avoid all perverse talk;
stay far from corrupt speech.*

Proverbs 4:24 NLT

GUARD YOUR SPEECH

Pleasant words are a honeycomb:
sweet to the taste and health to the body.

Proverbs 16:24 Holman CSB

Think . . . pause . . . then speak: How wise is the woman who can communicate in this way. But all too often, in the rush to have ourselves heard, we speak first and think next . . . with unfortunate results.

God's Word reminds us that "Reckless words pierce like a sword, but the tongue of the wise brings healing" (Proverbs 12:18 NIV). If we seek to be a source of encouragement to friends and family, then we must measure our words carefully. Words are important: They can hurt or heal. Words can uplift us or discourage us and reckless words, spoken in haste, cannot be erased.

Today, seek to encourage all who cross your path. Measure your words carefully. Speak wisely, not impulsively. Use words of kindness and praise, not words of anger or derision. Remember that you have the power to heal others or to injure them, to lift others up or to hold them back. When you lift them up, your wisdom will bring healing and comfort to a world that needs both.

Be gracious in your speech.
The goal is to bring out the best in others
in a conversation, not put them down,
not cut them out.

Colossians 4:6 MSG

A TIP FOR GUARDING YOUR HEART

Words, words, words . . . are important, important, important! So make sure that you think first and speak next. Otherwise, you may give the greatest speech you wish you'd never made!

WORDS OF WISDOM

We will always experience regret when we live for the moment and do not weigh our words and deeds before we give them life.

Lisa Bevere

Every word we speak, every action we take, has an effect on the totality of humanity. No one can escape that privilege—or that responsibility.

Laurie Beth Jones

The things that we feel most deeply we ought to learn to be silent about, at least until we have talked them over thoroughly with God.

Elisabeth Elliot

When you talk, choose the very same words that you would use if Jesus were looking over your shoulder. Because He is.

Marie T. Freeman

The battle of the tongue is won not in the mouth, but in the heart.

Annie Chapman

GOD'S WORDS OF WISDOM

So then, rid yourselves of all evil, all lying, hypocrisy, jealousy, and evil speech. As newborn babies want milk, you should want the pure and simple teaching. By it you can grow up and be saved.

1 Peter 2:1–2 NCV

To everything there is a season . . . a time to keep silence, and a time to speak.

Ecclesiastes 3:1,7 KJV

Watch the way you talk. Let nothing foul or dirty come out of your mouth. Say only what helps, each word a gift.

Ephesians 4:29 MSG

If anyone thinks he is religious, without controlling his tongue but deceiving his heart, his religion is useless.

James 1:26 Holman CSB

SUMMING IT UP

God understands the importance of the words you speak . . . and so must you.

GUARD YOUR WORDS BY STRIVING TO BE PATIENT

Always be humble, gentle, and patient,
accepting each other in love.

Ephesians 4:2 NCV

Are you a woman in a hurry? If so, you're probably not the only one in your neighborhood. We human beings are, by our very nature, impatient. We are impatient with others, impatient with ourselves, and impatient with our Creator. We want things to happen according to our own timetables, but our Heavenly Father may have other plans. That's why we must learn the art of patience.

All too often, we are unwilling to trust God's perfect timing. We allow ourselves to become apprehensive and anxious as we wait nervously for God to act. Usually, we know what we want, and we know precisely when we want it: right now, if not sooner. But, when God's plans differ from our own, we must train ourselves to trust in His infinite wisdom and in His infinite love.

As people living in a fast-paced world, many of us find that waiting quietly for God is quite troubling. But in our better moments, we realize that patience is not only a virtue, but it is also a commandment from the Creator.

Psalm 37:7 makes it clear that we should "Be still before the Lord and wait patiently for Him" (NIV). But ours is a generation that usually places little value on stillness and patience. No matter. God instructs us to be patient in all things, and we must obey Him or suffer the consequences of His displeasure.

We must be patient with our families, with our friends, and with ourselves. We must also be patient with our Heavenly Father as He shapes our world (and our lives) in accordance with His timetable, not our own. And that's as it should be. After all, think how patient God has been with us.

A TIP FOR GUARDING YOUR HEART

God has been patient with you . . . now it's your turn to be patient with others.

WORDS OF WISDOM

Let me encourage you to continue to wait with faith. God may not perform a miracle, but He is trustworthy to touch you and make you whole where there used to be a hole.

Lisa Whelchel

Waiting is the hardest kind of work, but God knows best, and we may joyfully leave all in His hands.

Lottie Moon

Wisdom always waits for the right time to act, while emotion always pushes for action right now.

Joyce Meyer

How do you wait upon the Lord? First you must learn to sit at His feet and take time to listen to His words.

Kay Arthur

When we read of the great Biblical leaders, we see that it was not uncommon for God to ask them to wait, not just a day or two, but for years, until God was ready for them to act.

Gloria Gaither

GOD'S WORDS OF WISDOM

We urge you, brethren, admonish the unruly, encourage the fainthearted, help the weak, be patient with everyone.

1 Thessalonians 5:14 NASB

Yet the Lord longs to be gracious to you; he rises to show you compassion. For the Lord is a God of justice. Blessed are all who wait for him!

Isaiah 30:18 NIV

Wait on the Lord; Be of good courage, and He shall strengthen your heart; Wait, I say, on the Lord!

Psalm 27:14 NKJV

The Lord is wonderfully good to those who wait for him and seek him. So it is good to wait quietly for salvation from the Lord.

Lamentations 3:25-26 NLT

SUMMING IT UP

When you learn to be more patient with others, you'll make your world—and your heart—a better place.

GUARD YOUR WORDS BY CELEBRATING LIFE

This is the day the Lord has made;
we will rejoice and be glad in it.

Psalm 118:24 NKJV

D o you celebrate the gifts God has given you? Do you pray without ceasing? Do you rejoice in the beauty of God's glorious creation? You should. But perhaps, as a busy woman living in a demanding world, you have been slow to count your gifts and even slower to give thanks to the Giver.

As God's children, we are all blessed beyond measure, and we should celebrate His blessings every day that we live. The gifts we receive from God are multiplied when we share them with others. Today is a non-renewable resource—once it's gone, it's gone forever. Our responsibility—as believers—is to give thanks for God's gifts and then use them in the service of God's will and in the service of His people.

God has blessed us beyond measure, and we owe Him everything, including our praise. And let us remember that for those of us who have been saved by God's only begotten Son, every day is a cause for celebration.

Shout for joy to the Lord, all the earth.
Worship the Lord with gladness;
come before him with joyful songs.

Psalm 100:1-2 NIV

A TIP FOR GUARDING YOUR HEART

If you don't feel like celebrating, start counting your blessings. Before long, you'll realize that you have plenty of reasons to celebrate.

WORDS OF WISDOM

Christ is the secret, the source, the substance, the center, and the circumference of all true and lasting gladness.

Mrs. Charles E. Cowman

Each one of us is responsible for our own happiness. If we choose to allow ourselves to become miserable and unhappy, the problem is ours, not someone else's.

Joyce Meyer

With God, life is eternal—both in quality and length. There is no joy comparable to the joy of discovering something new from God, about God. If the continuing life is a life of joy, we will go on discovering, learning.

Eugenia Price

If you can forgive the person you were, accept the person you are, and believe in the person you will become, you are headed for joy. So celebrate your life.

Barbara Johnson

GOD'S WORDS OF WISDOM

Celebrate God all day, every day. I mean, revel in him!

Philippians 4:4 MSG

David and the whole house of Israel were celebrating with all their might before the Lord, with songs and with harps, lyres, tambourines, sistrums and cymbals.

2 Samuel 6:5 NIV

At the dedication of the wall of Jerusalem, the Levites were sought out from where they lived and were brought to Jerusalem to celebrate joyfully the dedication with songs of thanksgiving and with the music of cymbals, harps and lyres.

Nehemiah 12:27 NIV

A happy heart is like a continual feast.

Proverbs 15:15 NCV

SUMMING IT UP

God has given you the gift of life (here on earth) and the promise of eternal life (in heaven). Now, He wants you to celebrate those gifts.

GUARD YOUR WORDS AGAINST THE TEMPTATION TO JUDGE

Do not judge, and you will not be judged.
Do not condemn, and you will not be condemned.
Forgive, and you will be forgiven.

Luke 6:37 Holman CSB

E ven the most devoted Christians may fall prey to a powerful yet subtle temptation: the temptation to judge others. But as Christians, we are commanded to refrain from such behavior. The warning of Matthew 7:1 is clear: "Judge not, that ye be not judged" (KJV). Yet, as fallible, imperfect human beings living in a stressful world, we are sorely tempted to do otherwise.

As Jesus came upon a young woman who had been condemned by the Pharisees, He spoke not only to the crowd that was gathered there, but also to all generations when He warned, "He that is without sin among you, let him first cast a stone at her" (John 8:7 KJV). Christ's message is clear, and it applies not only to the Pharisees of ancient times, but also to us.

We have all fallen short of God's commandments, and none of us, therefore, are qualified to "cast the first stone." Thankfully, God has forgiven us and we, too, must forgive others. As Christian believers, we are warned that to judge others is to invite fearful consequences: To the extent we judge others, so, too, will we be judged by God. Let us refrain, then, from judging our neighbors. Instead, let us forgive them and love them in the same way that God has forgiven us.

A TIP FOR GUARDING YOUR HEART

Your ability to judge others requires a divine insight that you simply don't have. So do everybody (including yourself) a favor: don't judge.

WORDS OF WISDOM

Judging draws the judgment of others.

Catherine Marshall

Perhaps the greatest blessing that religious inheritance can bestow is an open mind, one that can listen without judging.

Kathleen Norris

Only Christ can free us from the prison of legalism, and then only if we are willing to be freed.

Madeleine L'Engle

Don't judge other people more harshly than you want God to judge you.

Marie T. Freeman

A little kindly advice is better than a great deal of scolding.

Fanny Crosby

GOD'S WORDS OF WISDOM

▼

You, therefore, have no excuse, you who pass judgment on someone else, for at whatever point you judge the other, you are condemning yourself.

Romans 2:1 NIV

Speak and act as those who will be judged by the law of freedom. For judgment is without mercy to the one who hasn't shown mercy. Mercy triumphs over judgment.

James 2:12-13 Holman CSB

Therefore judge nothing before the time, until the Lord comes, who will both bring to light the hidden things of darkness and reveal the counsels of the hearts. Then each one's praise will come from God.

1 Corinthians 4:5 NKJV

SUMMING IT UP

To the extent you judge others, so, too, will you be judged. So you must, to the best of your ability, refrain from judgmental thoughts and words.

GUARD YOUR WORDS BY BEING KIND

Carry each other's burdens,
and in this way you will fulfill the law of Christ.

Galatians 6:2 NIV

Sometimes, when we feel happy or generous, we find it easy to be kind. Other times, when we are discouraged or tired, we can scarcely summon the energy to utter a single kind word. But, God's commandment is clear: He intends that we make the conscious choice to treat others with kindness and respect, no matter our circumstances, no matter our emotions.

For Christians, kindness is not an option; it is a commandment. In the Gospel of Matthew, Jesus declares, "In everything, therefore, treat people the same way you want them to treat you, for this is the Law and the Prophets" (Matthew 7:12 NASB). Jesus did not say, "In some things, treat people as you wish to be treated." And, He did not say, "From time to time, treat others with kindness." Christ said that we should treat others as we wish to be treated "in everything." This, of course, is a difficult task, but as Christians, we are commanded to do our best.

Today, as you consider all the things that Christ has done in your life, honor Him by being a little kinder than necessary. Honor Him by slowing down long enough to offer encouragement to someone who needs it. Honor Him by picking up the phone and calling a distant friend . . . for no reason other than to say, "I'm thinking of you." Honor Christ with your good words and your good deeds. Jesus expects no less, and He deserves no less.

Be ye therefore merciful,
as your Father also is merciful.

Luke 6:36 KJV

A TIP FOR GUARDING YOUR HEART

Kindness matters: When you make the decision to be a genuinely kind person, you'll make decisions that improve your own life and the lives of your family and friends.

WORDS OF WISDOM

Kindness in this world will do much to help others, not only to come into the light, but also to grow in grace day by day.

Fanny Crosby

Let no one ever come to you without leaving better and happier. Be the living expression of God's kindness: kindness in your face, kindness in your eyes, kindness in your smile.

Mother Teresa

It is one of the most beautiful compensations of life that no one can sincerely try to help another without helping herself.

Barbara Johnson

It doesn't take monumental feats to make the world a better place. It can be as simple as letting someone go ahead of you in a grocery line.

Barbara Johnson

When we Christians are too busy to care for each other, we're simply too busy for our own good . . . and for God's.

Marie T. Freeman

GOD'S WORDS OF WISDOM

Show respect for all people. Love the brothers and sisters of God's family.

1 Peter 2:17 ICB

May the Lord cause you to increase and abound in love for one another, and for all people.

1 Thessalonians 3:12 NASB

And be ye kind one to another, tenderhearted, forgiving one another, even as God for Christ's sake hath forgiven you.

Ephesians 4:32 KJV

Verily I say unto you, Inasmuch as ye have done it unto one of the least of these my brethren, ye have done it unto me.

Matthew 25:40 KJV

SUMMING IT UP

Kind words have echoes that last a lifetime and beyond.

GUARD YOUR WORDS WITH AN ENTHUSIASTIC HEART

Whatever you do, do it enthusiastically,
as something done for the Lord and not for men.

Colossians 3:23 Holman CSB

Are you enthusiastic about your life and your faith? Hopefully so. But if your zest for life has waned, it is now time to redirect your efforts and recharge your spiritual batteries. And that means refocusing your priorities (by putting God first) and counting your blessings (instead of your troubles).

Nothing is more important than your wholehearted commitment to your Creator and to His only begotten Son. Your faith must never be an afterthought; it must be your ultimate priority, your ultimate possession, and your ultimate passion. When you become passionate about your faith, you'll become passionate about your life, too.

Genuine, heartfelt, enthusiastic Christianity is contagious. If you enjoy a life-altering relationship with God, that relationship will have an impact on others—perhaps a profound impact.

Do you see each day as a glorious opportunity to serve God and to do His will? Are you enthused about life, or do you struggle through each day giving scarcely a thought to God's blessings? Are you constantly praising God for His gifts, and are you sharing His Good News with the world? And are you excited about the possibilities for service that God has placed before you, whether at home, at work, at church, or at school? You should be.

You are the recipient of Christ's sacrificial love. Accept it enthusiastically and share it fervently. Jesus deserves your enthusiasm; the world deserves it; and you deserve the experience of sharing it.

A TIP FOR GUARDING YOUR HEART

Don't wait for enthusiasm to find you . . . go looking for it. Look at your life and your relationships as exciting adventures. Don't wait for life to spice itself; spice things up yourself.

WORDS OF WISDOM

Enthusiasm, like the flu, is contagious—we get it from one another.

Barbara Johnson

Finding your passion is the single most important ingredient for changing your world.

Nicole Johnson

The idea of always playing it safe, never venturing out of our comfort zone, and refusing to broaden the borders of our experience is stultifying.

Marilyn Meberg

It's ironic that one of the best remedies for impending burnout is to give yourself away—to pick out one time and place each week where you can stretch out your hands for the pure joy of doing it.

Liz Curtis Higgs

GOD'S WORDS OF WISDOM

Whatever work you do, do your best, because you are going to the grave, where there is no working . . . .

Ecclesiastes 9:10 NCV

I have seen that there is nothing better than for a person to enjoy his activities, because that is his reward. For who can enable him to see what will happen after he dies?

Ecclesiastes 3:22 Holman CSB

Do your work with enthusiasm. Work as if you were serving the Lord, not as if you were serving only men and women.

Ephesians 6:7 NCV

Never be lazy in your work, but serve the Lord enthusiastically.

Romans 12:11 NLT

SUMMING IT UP

When you become genuinely enthused about your life and your faith, you'll guard your heart and improve your life.

GUARD YOUR WORDS AGAINST BITTERNESS

Get rid of all bitterness, rage, anger, harsh words,
and slander, as well as all types of malicious behavior.
Instead, be kind to each other, tenderhearted, forgiving
one another, just as God through Christ has forgiven you.
Ephesians 4:31-32 NLT

Even the most mild-mannered women will, on occasion, have reason to become angry with the inevitable shortcomings of family members and friends. But wise women are quick to forgive others, just as God has forgiven them.

The commandment to forgive others is clearly a part of God's Word, but oh how difficult a commandment it can be to follow. Because we are imperfect beings, we are quick to anger, quick to blame, slow to forgive, and even slower to forget. No matter. Even when forgiveness is difficult, God's instructions are straightforward: As Christians who have received the gift of forgiveness, we must now share that gift with others.

If, in your heart, you hold bitterness against even a single person, forgive. If there exists even one person, alive or dead, whom you have not forgiven, follow God's commandment and His will for your life: forgive. If you are embittered against yourself for some past mistake or shortcoming, forgive. Then, to the best of your abilities, forget, and move on. Bitterness and regret are not part of God's plan for your life. Forgiveness is. And once you've forgiven others, you can then turn your thoughts to a far more pleasant subject: the incredibly bright future that God has promised.

Hatred stirs up trouble,
but love forgives all wrongs.

Proverbs 10:12 NCV

A TIP FOR GUARDING YOUR HEART

Holding a grudge? Drop it. Never expect other people to be more forgiving than you are. And remember: The best time to forgive is now.

WORDS OF WISDOM

Have you thought that your willingness to forgive is really your affirmation of the power of God to do you good?

Paula Rinehart

God gives us permission to forget our past and the understanding to live our present. He said He will remember our sins no more. (Psalm 103:11-12)

Serita Ann Jakes

God has been very gracious to me, for I never dwell upon anything wrong which a person has done to me, as to remember it afterwards. If I do remember it, I always see some other virtue in the person.

St. Teresa of Avila

Forgiveness is actually the best revenge because it not only sets us free from the person we forgive, but it frees us to move into all that God has in store for us.

Stormie Omartian

God expects us to forgive others as He has forgiven us; we are to follow His example by having a forgiving heart.

Vonette Bright

GOD'S WORDS OF WISDOM

Our Father is kind; you be kind. "Don't pick on people, jump on their failures, criticize their faults— unless, of course, you want the same treatment. Don't condemn those who are down; that hardness can boomerang. Be easy on people; you'll find life a lot easier."

Luke 6:36-37 MSG

Be even-tempered, content with second place, quick to forgive an offense. Forgive as quickly and completely as the Master forgave you. And regardless of what else you put on, wear love. It's your basic, all-purpose garment. Never be without it.

Colossians 3:13-14 MSG

Have mercy on me, O God, according to your unfailing love; according to your great compassion blot out my transgressions. Wash away all my iniquity and cleanse me from my sin.

Psalm 51:1-2 NIV

SUMMING IT UP

Forgiveness is its own reward. Bitterness is its own punishment. Guard your words and your thoughts accordingly.

GUARD YOUR WORDS WITH SILENCE

Be silent before the Lord and wait expectantly for Him.

Psalm 37:7 Holman CSB

Here's a simple prescription for guarding your heart: Carve out a little time for silence every day. Here in our noisy, 21st-century world, silence is highly underrated. Many of us can't even seem to walk from the front door to the street without a cell phone or an iPod in our ear. The world seems to grow louder day by day, and our senses seem to be invaded at every turn. But, if we allow the distractions of a clamorous society to separate us from God's peace, we do ourselves a profound disservice. So if we're wise, we make time each day for quiet reflection. And when we do, we are rewarded.

Do you take time each day for an extended period of silence? And during those precious moments, do you sincerely open your heart to your Creator? If so, you will be blessed. If not, then the struggles and stresses of everyday living may rob you of the peace that should rightfully be yours because of your personal relationship with Christ. So take time each day to quietly commune with your Creator. When you do, those moments of silence will enable you to participate more fully in the only source of peace that endures: God's peace.

Settle yourself in solitude,
and you will come upon Him in yourself.

St. Teresa of Avila

A TIP FOR GUARDING YOUR HEART

Want to talk to God? Then don't make Him shout. If you really want to hear from God, go to a quiet place and listen. If you keep listening long enough and carefully enough, He'll start talking.

WORDS OF WISDOM

Let your loneliness be transformed into a holy aloneness.
Sit still before the Lord. Remember Naomi's word to Ruth:
"Sit still, my daughter, until you see how the matter will
fall."

Elisabeth Elliot

Be still, and in the quiet moments, listen to the voice of
your heavenly Father. His words can renew your spirit—no
one knows you and your needs like He does.

Janet L. Weaver Smith

So wait before the Lord. Wait in the stillness. And in that
stillness, assurance will come to you. You will know that
you are heard; you will know that your Lord ponders the
voice of your humble desires; you will hear quiet words
spoken to you yourself, perhaps to your grateful surprise
and refreshment.

Amy Carmichael

Instead of waiting for the feeling, wait upon God. You
can do this by growing still and quiet, then expressing in
prayer what your mind knows is true about Him, even if
your heart doesn't feel it at this moment.

Shirley Dobson

GOD'S WORDS OF WISDOM

In quietness and trust is your strength.

Isaiah 30:15 NASB

Be still, and know that I am God.

Psalm 46:10 NKJV

I wait quietly before God, for my hope is in him.

Psalm 62:5 NLT

What's this? Fools out shopping for wisdom! They wouldn't recognize it if they saw it! One Who Knows Much Says Little.

Proverbs 17:16 MSG

Be silent before Me.

Isaiah 41:1 Holman CSB

SUMMING IT UP

Spend a few moments each day in silence. You owe it to your Creator . . . and to yourself.

GUARD YOUR WORDS BY BEING GRATEFUL

Give thanks to the Lord, for He is good;
His faithful love endures forever.

Psalm 106:1 Holman CSB

God has blessed us beyond measure, and we owe Him everything, including our constant praise. That's why thanksgiving should become a habit, a regular part of our daily routines. When we slow down and express our gratitude to the One who made us, we enrich our own lives and the lives of those around us.

Dietrich Bonhoeffer observed, "It is only with gratitude that life becomes rich." These words most certainly apply to you.

As a follower of Christ, you have been blessed beyond measure. God sent His only Son to die for you. And, God has given you the priceless gifts of eternal love and eternal life. You, in turn, should approach your Heavenly Father with reverence and gratitude.

Are you a thankful person? Do you appreciate the gifts that God has given you? And, do you demonstrate your gratitude by being a faithful steward of the gifts and talents that you have received from your Creator? You most certainly should be thankful. After all, when you stop to think about it, God has given you more blessings than you can count. So the question of the day is this: Will you thank your Heavenly Father . . . or will you spend your time and energy doing other things?

God is always listening—are you willing to say thanks? It's up to you, and the next move is yours.

Enter his gates with thanksgiving,
go into his courts with praise.
Give thanks to him and bless his name.

Psalm 100:4 NLT

A TIP FOR GUARDING YOUR HEART

By speaking words of thanksgiving and praise, you honor to the Father and you protect your heart against the twin evils of apathy and ingratitude.

WORDS OF WISDOM

God is worthy of our praise and is pleased when we come before Him with thanksgiving.

Shirley Dobson

The act of thanksgiving is a demonstration of the fact that you are going to trust and believe God.

Kay Arthur

Thanksgiving is good but Thanksliving is better.

Jim Gallery

Thanksgiving or complaining—these words express two contrastive attitudes of the souls of God's children in regard to His dealings with them. The soul that gives thanks can find comfort in everything; the soul that complains can find comfort in nothing.

Hannah Whitall Smith

One reason why we don't thank God for his answer to our prayer is that frequently we don't recognize them as being answers to our prayers. We just take his bountiful supply or dramatic action for granted when it comes.

Evelyn Christenson

GOD'S WORDS OF WISDOM

In everything give thanks; for this is the will of God in Christ Jesus for you.

1 Thessalonians 5:18 NKJV

Our prayers for you are always spilling over into thanksgivings. We can't quit thanking God our Father and Jesus our Messiah for you!

Colossians 1:3 MSG

My counsel for you is simple and straightforward: Just go ahead with what you've been given. You received Christ Jesus, the Master; now live him. You're deeply rooted in him. You're well constructed upon him. You know your way around the faith. Now do what you've been taught. School's out; quit studying the subject and start living it! And let your living spill over into thanksgiving.

Colossians 2:6-7 MSG

SUMMING IT UP

You owe God everything . . . including your thanks.

PART 2

GUARD
YOUR EYES

*Look straight ahead,
and fix your eyes on what lies before you.*

Proverbs 4:25 NLT

GUARD YOUR EYES AGAINST THE WORLD'S MANY TEMPTATIONS

Put on the whole armor of God,
that you may be able to stand against the wiles of the devil.

Ephesians 6:11 NKJV

Here in the 21st century, temptations are now completely and thoroughly woven into the fabric of everyday life. Seductive images are everywhere; subtle messages tell you that it's okay to sin "just a little"; and to make matters even worse, society doesn't just seem to endorse godlessness, it actually seems to reward it. Society spews forth a wide range of messages, all of which imply that it's okay to rebel against God. These messages, of course, are extremely dangerous and completely untrue.

How can you stand up against society's tidal wave of temptations? By learning to direct your thoughts and your eyes in ways that are pleasing to God . . . and by relying upon Him to deliver you from the evils that threaten you. And here's the good news: The Creator has promised (not implied, not suggested, not insinuated—He has promised!) that with His help, you can resist every single temptation that confronts you.

When it comes to fighting Satan, you are never alone. God is always with you, and if you do your part He will do His part. But what, precisely, is your part? A good starting point is simply learning how to recognize the subtle temptations that surround you. The images of immorality are ubiquitous, and they're intended to hijack your mind, your heart, your pocketbook, your life, and your soul. Don't let them do it.

Satan is both industrious and creative; he's working 24/7, and he's causing pain, heartache, trauma, and tragedy in more ways than ever before. As a Christian, you must remain watchful and strong—starting today, and ending never.

A TIP FOR GUARDING YOUR HEART

You live in a Temptation Generation: You can find temptation in lots of places. Your job is to avoid those places!

WORDS OF WISDOM

Do not fight the temptation in detail. Turn from it. Look ONLY at your Lord. Sing. Read. Work.

Amy Carmichael

Because Christ has faced our every temptation without sin, we never face a temptation that has no door of escape.

Beth Moore

Temptation is not a sin. Even Jesus was tempted. The Lord Jesus gives you the strength needed to resist temptation.

Corrie ten Boom

The devil's most devilish when respectable.

Elizabeth Barrett Browning

In the Garden of Gethsemane, Jesus went through agony of soul in His efforts to resist the temptation to do what He felt like doing rather than what He knew was God's will for Him.

Joyce Meyer

GOD'S WORDS OF WISDOM

Be sober! Be on the alert! Your adversary the Devil is prowling around like a roaring lion, looking for anyone he can devour.

1 Peter 5:8 Holman CSB

So let God work his will in you. Yell a loud no to the Devil and watch him scamper. Say a quiet yes to God and he'll be there in no time. Quit dabbling in sin. Purify your inner life. Quit playing the field.

James 4:7-8 MSG

For we do not have a High Priest who cannot sympathize with our weaknesses, but was in all points tempted as we are, yet without sin. Let us therefore come boldly to the throne of grace, that we may obtain mercy and find grace to help in time of need.

Hebrews 4:15-16 NKJV

SUMMING IT UP

Because you live in a temptation-filled world, you must guard your eyes, your thoughts, and your heart—all day, every day.

GUARD YOUR EYES AGAINST MATERIALISM

And He told them, "Watch out and be on guard against all greed, because one's life is not in the abundance of his possessions."

Luke 12:15 Holman CSB

How important are your material possessions? Not as important as you might think. In the life of a committed Christian, material possessions should play a rather small role. In fact, when we become overly enamored with the things we own, we needlessly distance ourselves from the peace that God offers to those who place Him at the center of their lives.

Of course, we all need the basic necessities of life, but once we meet those needs for ourselves and for our families, the piling up of possessions creates more problems than it solves. Our real riches, of course, are not of this world. We are never really rich until we are rich in spirit.

Do you find yourself wrapped up in the concerns of the material world? If so, it's time to reorder your priorities by turning your thoughts and your prayers to more important matters. And, it's time to begin storing up riches that will endure throughout eternity: the spiritual kind.

He who trusts in his riches will fall,
but the righteous will flourish . . . .

Proverbs 11:28 NKJV

A TIP FOR GUARDING YOUR HEART

Too much stuff doesn't ensure happiness. In fact, having too much stuff can actually prevent happiness.

WORDS OF WISDOM

We are made spiritually lethargic by a steady diet of materialism.

Mary Morrison Suggs

Outside appearances, things like the clothes you wear or the car you drive, are important to other people but totally unimportant to God. Trust God.

Marie T. Freeman

Greed is enslaving. The more you have, the more you want—until eventually avarice consumes you.

Kay Arthur

As faithful stewards of what we have, ought we not to give earnest thought to our staggering surplus?

Elisabeth Elliot

It's sobering to contemplate how much time, effort, sacrifice, compromise, and attention we give to acquiring and increasing our supply of something that is totally insignificant in eternity.

Anne Graham Lotz

GOD'S WORDS OF WISDOM

Do not love the world or the things in the world. If anyone loves the world, the love of the Father is not in him.

1 John 2:15 NKJV

For what will it profit a man if he gains the whole world, and loses his own soul? Or what will a man give in exchange for his soul?

Mark 8:36-37 NKJV

For the mind-set of the flesh is death, but the mind-set of the Spirit is life and peace.

Romans 8:6 Holman CSB

Since we entered the world penniless and will leave it penniless, if we have bread on the table and shoes on our feet, that's enough.

1 Timothy 6:7-8 MSG

SUMMING IT UP

Material possessions may seem appealing at first, but they pale in comparison to the spiritual gifts that God gives to those who put Him first. Count yourself among that number.

GUARD YOUR EYES BY CLOSING THEM AT A SENSIBLE HOUR

Come to me, all you who are weary and burdened, and I will give you rest. Take my yoke upon you and learn from me, for I am gentle and humble in heart, and you will find rest for your souls. For my yoke is easy and my burden is light.

Matthew 11:28-30 NIV

Even the most energetic Christians can, from time to time, find themselves running on empty. The demands of daily life can drain us of our strength and rob us of the joy that is rightfully ours in Christ. When we find ourselves tired, discouraged, or worse, there is a source from which we can draw the power needed to recharge our spiritual batteries. That source is God.

God intends that His children lead joyous lives filled with abundance and peace. But sometimes, abundance and peace seem very far away. It is then that we must turn to God for renewal, and when we do, He will restore us.

Physical exhaustion is God's way of telling us to slow down. God expects us to work hard, of course, but He also intends for us to rest. When we fail to take the rest that we need, we do a disservice to ourselves and to our families.

We live in a world that tempts us to stay up late—very late. But too much late-night TV, combined with too little sleep, is a prescription for exhaustion.

Are your physical or spiritual batteries running low? Is your energy on the wane? Are your emotions frayed? If so, it's time to turn your thoughts and your prayers to God. And when you're finished, it's probably time to turn off the lights and go to bed!

A TIP FOR GUARDING YOUR HEART

Getting enough sleep? If you find yourself short on patience, perhaps you're also short on sleep. If so, turn off the TV and go to bed. As your energy returns, so will your patience.

WORDS OF WISDOM

Life is strenuous. See that your clock does not run down.

Mrs. Charles E. Cowman

Taking care of yourself physically really helps emotionally. People who get a lot of sleep, who do the things that relieve stress, can withstand a lot of stress.

Laura Bush

Jesus taught us by example to get out of the rat race and recharge our batteries.

Barbara Johnson

Come, come, come unto Me, weary and sore distressed; come, come, come unto Me, come unto Me and rest.

Fanny Crosby

One reason so much American Christianity is a mile wide and an inch deep is that Christians are simply tired. Sometimes you need to kick back and rest for Jesus' sake.

Dennis Swanberg

GOD'S WORDS OF WISDOM

And the apostles gathered themselves together unto Jesus, and told him all things, both what they had done, and what they had taught. And he said unto them, Come ye yourselves apart into a desert place, and rest a while.

Mark 6:30-31 Holman CSB

I said to myself, "Relax and rest. God has showered you with blessings."

Psalm 116:7 MSG

I find rest in God; only he gives me hope.

Psalm 62:5 NCV

But those who wait on the Lord Shall renew their strength; They shall mount up with wings like eagles, They shall run and not be weary, They shall walk and not faint.

Isaiah 40:31 NKJV

SUMMING IT UP

Your body, which is a priceless gift from God, needs a sensible amount of sleep each night. Schedule your life accordingly.

GUARD YOUR EYES AGAINST ENVY

*But if you harbor bitter envy and selfish ambition
in your hearts, do not boast about it or deny the truth.
Such "wisdom" does not come down from heaven but is
earthly, unspiritual, of the devil. For where you have
envy and selfish ambition,
there you find disorder and every evil practice.*

James 3:14-17 NIV

Because we are frail, imperfect human beings, we are sometimes envious of others. But God's Word warns us that envy is sin. Thus, we must guard ourselves against the natural tendency to feel resentment and jealousy when other people experience good fortune.

As believers, we have absolutely no reason to be envious of any people on earth. After all, as Christians we are already recipients of the greatest gift in all creation: God's grace. We have been promised the gift of eternal life through God's only begotten Son, and we must count that gift as our most precious possession.

Rather than succumbing to the sin of envy, we should focus on the marvelous things that God has done for us—starting with Christ's sacrifice. And we must refrain from preoccupying ourselves with the blessings that God has chosen to give others.

So here's a surefire formula for a happier, healthier life: Count your own blessings and let your neighbors count theirs. It's the godly way to live.

Let us not become boastful,
challenging one another, envying one another.

Galatians 5:26 NASB

A TIP FOR GUARDING YOUR HEART

You can be envious, or you can be happy, but you can't be both. Envy and happiness can't live at the same time in the same brain.

WORDS OF WISDOM

What God asks, does, or requires of others is not my business; it is His.

Kay Arthur

Discontent dries up the soul.

Elisabeth Elliot

If we find ourselves imprisoned, then, we may be sure of this: that it is not our earthly environment that constitutes our prison-house, for the soul's wings scorn all paltry bars and walls of earth's making. The only thing that can really imprison the soul is something that hinders its upward flight.

Hannah Whitall Smith

Joy is the keynote of the Christian life. It is not something that happens. It is a gift, given to us in the coming of Christ.

Elisabeth Elliot

GOD'S WORDS OF WISDOM

Therefore, laying aside all malice, all deceit, hypocrisy, envy, and all evil speaking, as newborn babes, desire the pure milk of the word, that you may grow thereby.

1 Peter 2:1-2 NKJV

You shall not covet your neighbor's house; you shall not covet your neighbor's wife, nor his male servant, nor his female servant, nor his ox, nor his donkey, nor anything that is your neighbor's.

Exodus 20:17 NKJV

I have told you these things, so that in me you may have peace. In this world you will have trouble. But take heart! I have overcome the world.

John 16:33 NIV

SUMMING IT UP

Envy is a sin, a sin that robs you of contentment and peace. So you must refuse to let feelings of envy invade your thoughts or your heart.

GUARD YOUR HEART BY LOOKING STRAIGHT AHEAD

Look straight ahead, and fix your eyes on what lies before you.

Proverbs 4:25 NLT

You know that you should guard your heart against immorality, but sometimes it's hard to do. Have you noticed that the world is filled to the brim with temptations? Unless you've been living the life of a hermit, you've observed that temptations, both great and small, are everywhere.

Some temptations are small; eating a second scoop of ice cream, for example, is tempting, but not very dangerous. Other temptations, however, are not nearly so harmless. And when you are faced with temptations that threaten to compromise the moral standards that have been spelled out in God's Holy Word, you must run (not walk) in the opposite direction.

The devil is working 24 hours a day, and he's causing pain and heartache in more ways than ever before. Thankfully, in the battle against Satan, you are never alone. God is always with you, and He gives you the power to resist temptation whenever you ask Him for the strength to do so.

In a letter to believers, Peter offered a stern warning: "Your adversary the devil walks about like a roaring lion, seeking whom he may devour" (1 Peter 5:8 NKJV). As a believer, you must heed that warning, and you must behave accordingly.

Pursue peace with all people, and holiness, without which no one will see the Lord.

Hebrews 12:14 NKJV

A TIP FOR GUARDING YOUR HEART

Always avoid people and places that might tempt you to disobey God's commandments.

WORDS OF WISDOM

We are in desperate need for women of faith who are willing to courageously stand against sin and stand for righteousness.

Susan Hunt

The soul of a righteous person is nothing but a paradise, in which, as God tells us, he takes his delight.

St. Teresa of Avila

Christ has made my soul beautiful with the jewels of grace and virtue. I belong to Him whom the angels serve.

St. Agnes

Our progress in holiness depends on God and ourselves— on God's grace and on our will to be holy.

Mother Teresa

Holiness is not God's asking us to be "good"; it is an invitation to be "His."

Lisa Bevere

GOD'S WORDS OF WISDOM

Real wisdom, God's wisdom, begins with a holy life and is characterized by getting along with others. It is gentle and reasonable, overflowing with mercy and blessings, not hot one day and cold the next, not two-faced.

James 3:17 MSG

Since everything here today might well be gone tomorrow, do you see how essential it is to live a holy life?

2 Peter 3:11 MSG

But now you must be holy in everything you do, just as God— who chose you to be his children—is holy. For he himself has said, "You must be holy because I am holy."

1 Peter 1:15-16 NLT

You will teach me how to live a holy life. Being with you will fill me with joy; at your right hand I will find pleasure forever.

Psalm 16:11 NCV

SUMMING IT UP

Sin has the power to destroy the things you hold dear, starting, of course, with your family. So you must never let down your guard.

PART 3

GUARD
YOUR STEPS

Mark out a straight path for your feet;
then stick to the path and stay safe.
Don't get sidetracked;
keep your feet from following evil.

Proverbs 4:26-27 NLT

GUARD YOUR HEART BY WATCHING YOUR STEPS

Mark out a straight path for your feet;
then stick to the path and stay safe.

Proverbs 4:26 NLT

If you desire to guard your heart, you must choose a path that is pleasing to God, but you'll be tempted to choose a different path. If you're like most people, you seek the admiration of your neighbors, your coworkers, and your family members. But the eagerness to please others should never overshadow your eagerness to please God. If you seek to fulfill the purposes that God has in store for you, then you must be a "doer of the word." And how can you do so? By putting God first.

The words of Matthew 6:33 make it clear: "But seek first the kingdom of God and His righteousness, and all these things will be provided for you" (Holman CSB). God has given you a priceless guidebook, an indispensable tool for "seeking His kingdom." That tool, of course, is the

Holy Bible. It contains thorough instructions which, if followed, lead to fulfillment, righteousness, and salvation.

But for those who would ignore God's Word, Martin Luther issued this warning: "You may as well quit reading and hearing the Word of God and give it to the devil if you do not desire to live according to it." He understood that obedience leads to abundance just as surely as disobedience leads to disaster; you should understand it, too.

Each new day presents countless opportunities to put God in first place . . . or not. When you honor Him by living according to His commandments, you earn the abundance and peace that He promises. But, if you ignore God's teachings, you will inevitably bring needless suffering upon yourself and your family.

Would you like a time-tested formula for successful living? Here it is: Don't just listen to God's Word, live by it. Does this sound too simple? Perhaps it is simple, but it is also the only way to reap the marvelous riches that God has in store for you.

A Tip for Guarding Your Heart

Ask yourself if your behavior has been radically changed by your unfolding relationship with God. If the answer is to this question is unclear to you—or if the honest answer is a resounding no—think of a single step you can take, a positive change in your life, that will bring you closer to your Creator.

WORDS OF WISDOM

We have a decision to make—to turn away from sin or to be miserable and suffer the consequences of continual disobedience.

Vonette Bright

We are to leave an impression on all those we meet that communicates whose we are and what kingdom we represent.

Lisa Bevere

Although God causes all things to work together for good for His children, He still holds us accountable for our behavior.

Kay Arthur

There may be no trumpet sound or loud applause when we make a right decision, just a calm sense of resolution and peace.

Gloria Gaither

Study the Bible and observe how the persons behaved and how God dealt with them. There is explicit teaching on every condition of life.

Corrie ten Boom

GOD'S WORDS OF WISDOM

Light shines on the godly, and joy on those who do right. May all who are godly be happy in the Lord and praise his holy name.

Psalm 97:11-12 NLT

Even a child is known by his actions, by whether his conduct is pure and right.

Proverbs 20:11 NIV

He who has My commandments and keeps them, it is he who loves Me. And he who loves Me will be loved by My Father, and I will love him and manifest Myself to him.

John 14:21 NKJV

Who is wise and understanding among you? Let him show by good conduct that his works are done in the meekness of wisdom.

James 3:13 NKJV

SUMMING IT UP

How can you guard your steps? By walking with Jesus every day of your life.

GUARD YOUR STEPS BY ASKING GOD

So I say to you, keep asking, and it will be given to you.
Keep searching, and you will find.
Keep knocking, and the door will be opened to you.

Luke 11:9 Holman CSB

I f you sincerely want to guard your heart, you should ask for God's help. How often do you ask God for His help and His wisdom? Occasionally? Intermittently? Whenever you experience a crisis? Hopefully not. Hopefully, you've acquired the habit of asking for God's assistance early and often. And hopefully, you have learned to seek His guidance in every aspect of your life.

Jesus made it clear to His disciples: They should petition God to meet their needs. So should you. Genuine, heartfelt prayer produces powerful changes in you and in your world. When you lift your heart to God, you open yourself to a never-ending source of divine wisdom and infinite love.

God can do great things through you if you have the courage to ask Him (and the determination to keep asking Him). But don't expect Him to do all the work. When you do your part, He will do His part—and when He does, you can expect miracles to happen.

The Bible promises that God will guide you if you let Him. Your job is to let Him. But sometimes, you will be tempted to do otherwise. Sometimes, you'll be tempted to go along with the crowd; other times, you'll be tempted to do things your way, not God's way. When you feel those temptations, resist them.

God has promised that when you ask for His help, He will not withhold it. So ask. Ask Him to meet the needs of your day. Ask Him to lead you, to protect you, and to correct you. Then, trust the answers He gives.

God stands at the door and waits. When you knock, He opens. When you ask, He answers. Your task, of course, is to make God a full partner in every aspect of your life—and to seek His guidance prayerfully, confidently, and often.

A TIP FOR GUARDING YOUR HEART

Today, think of a specific need that is weighing heavily on your heart. Then, spend a few quiet moments asking God for His guidance and for His help.

WORDS OF WISDOM

When will we realize that we're not troubling God with our questions and concerns? His heart is open to hear us—his touch nearer than our next thought—as if no one in the world existed but us. Our very personal God wants to hear from us personally.

Gigi Graham Tchividjian

God will help us become the people we are meant to be, if only we will ask Him.

Hannah Whitall Smith

When trials come your way—as inevitably they will—do not run away. Run to your God and Father.

Kay Arthur

Often I have made a request of God with earnest pleadings even backed up with Scripture, only to have Him say "No" because He had something better in store.

Ruth Bell Graham

By asking in Jesus' name, we're making a request not only in His authority, but also for His interests and His benefit.

Shirley Dobson

GOD'S WORDS OF WISDOM

*Do not worry about anything, but pray and ask God for
everything you need, always giving thanks.*

Philippians 4:6 NCV

You do not have, because you do not ask God.

James 4:2 NIV

*You did not choose me, but I chose you and appointed you to
go and bear fruit—fruit that will last. Then the Father will give
you whatever you ask in my name.*

John 15:16 NIV

*Don't worry about anything, but in everything, through prayer
and petition with thanksgiving, let your requests be made
known to God.*

Philippians 4:6 Holman CSB

SUMMING IT UP

If you sincerely want to guard your steps, ask for God's
help.

GUARD YOUR STEPS WITH DAILY DEVOTIONALS

*Every morning he wakes me. He teaches me to listen
like a student. The Lord God helps me learn . . . .*

Isaiah 50:4-5 NCV

Each new day is a gift from God, and if we are wise, we will spend a few quiet moments each morning thanking the Giver. When we begin each day with heads bowed and hearts lifted, we remind ourselves of God's love, His protection, and His commandments. And if we are wise, we align our priorities for the coming day with the teachings and commandments that God has given us through His Holy Word.

The path to spiritual maturity unfolds day by day. Each day offers the opportunity to worship God, to ignore God, or to rebel against God. When we worship Him with our prayers, our words, our thoughts, and our actions, we are blessed by the richness of our relationship with the Father. But if we ignore God altogether or intentionally rebel against His commandments, we rob ourselves of His blessings.

Today offers yet another opportunity for spiritual growth. If you choose, you can seize that opportunity by obeying God's Word, by seeking His will, and by walking with His Son.

Are you seeking to change some aspect of your life? Do seek to improve the condition of your spiritual, physical, emotional, or financial health? If so, ask for God's help and ask for it many times each day . . . starting with your morning devotional.

Be still, and know that I am God.

Psalm 46:10 NKJV

A TIP FOR GUARDING YOUR HEART

If you're wise, you'll place a high priority on spending quiet time with God each day. If you can't find time for God, then it's time to give your "to-do" list a major overhaul.

WORDS OF WISDOM

How motivating it has been for me to view my early morning devotions as a time of retreat alone with Jesus, Who desires that I "come with Him by myself to a quiet place" in order to pray, read His Word, listen for His voice, and be renewed in my spirit.

Anne Graham Lotz

Every day has its own particular brand of holiness to discover and worship appropriately.

Annie Dillard

I think that God required the Israelites to gather manna every morning so that they would learn to come to Him daily.

Cynthia Heald

Faithful prayer warriors and devoted Bible lovers will tell you that their passion for disciplined quiet time with the Lord is not a sign of strength but an admission of weakness—a hard-earned realization that they are nothing on their own compared with who they are after they've been with him.

Doris Greig

GOD'S WORDS OF WISDOM

It is good to give thanks to the Lord, to sing praises to the Most High. It is good to proclaim your unfailing love in the morning, your faithfulness in the evening.

Psalm 92:1-2 NLT

Truly my soul silently waits for God; from Him comes my salvation.

Psalm 62:1 NKJV

May the words of my mouth and the thoughts of my heart be pleasing to you, O Lord, my rock and my redeemer.

Psalm 19:14 NLT

But grow in the grace and knowledge of our Lord and Savior Jesus Christ. To Him be the glory both now and to the day of eternity.

2 Peter 3:18 Holman CSB

SUMMING IT UP

You need a regular appointment with your Creator. God is ready to talk to you, and you should prepare yourself each morning to talk to Him.

GUARD YOUR STEPS AGAINST EVIL

Don't get sidetracked; keep your feet from following evil.

Proverbs 4:27 NLT

This world is God's creation, and it contains the wonderful fruits of His handiwork. But, the world also contains countless opportunities to stray from God's will. Temptations are everywhere, and the devil, it seems, never takes a day off. Our task, as believers, is to turn away from temptation and to place our lives squarely in the center of God's will.

In his letter to Jewish Christians, Peter offered a stern warning: "Your adversary, the devil, prowls around like a roaring lion, seeking someone to devour" (1 Peter 5:8 NASB). What was true in New Testament times is equally true in our own. Evil is indeed abroad in the world, and Satan continues to sow the seeds of destruction far and wide. In a very real sense, our world is at war: good versus evil, sin versus righteousness, hope versus suffering, praise versus apathy. As Christians, we must ensure that we place ourselves squarely on the right side of these conflicts: God's side. How can we do it? By thoughtfully studying God's Word, by regularly worshiping with fellow believers, and by guarding our hearts and minds against the subtle temptations of the enemy. When we do, we are protected.

> *Do not be conquered by evil,*
> *but conquer evil with good.*
>
> *Romans 12:21 Holman CSB*

A Tip for Guarding Your Heart

There is darkness in this world, but God's light can overpower any darkness.

WORDS OF WISDOM

We are in a continual battle with the spiritual forces of evil, but we will triumph when we yield to God's leading and call on His powerful presence in prayer.

Shirley Dobson

When we feel like the prey, a victim of evil pursuit, it's time for us to pray and take action against our predator.

Serita Ann Jakes

Where God's ministers are most successful, there the powers of darkness marshal their forces for the conflict.

Lottie Moon

Holiness has never been the driving force of the majority. It is, however, mandatory for anyone who wants to enter the kingdom.

Elisabeth Elliot

Light is stronger than darkness—darkness cannot "comprehend" or "overcome" it.

Anne Graham Lotz

GOD'S WORDS OF WISDOM

Be sober! Be on the alert! Your adversary the Devil is prowling around like a roaring lion, looking for anyone he can devour.

1 Peter 5:8 Holman CSB

Therefore, submit to God. But resist the Devil, and he will flee from you. Draw near to God, and He will draw near to you. Cleanse your hands, sinners, and purify your hearts, double-minded people!

James 4:7-8 Holman CSB

This High Priest of ours understands our weaknesses, for he faced all of the same temptations we do, yet he did not sin.

Hebrews 4:15 NLT

Do not fret because of evildoers; don't envy the wicked.

Proverbs 24:19 NLT

SUMMING IT UP

Evil exists, and it exists someplace not too far from you. You must guard your steps and your heart accordingly.

GUARD YOUR STEPS
WITH YOUR FAMILY

Choose for yourselves today the one you will worship . . . .
As for me and my family, we will worship the Lord.
Joshua 24:15 Holman CSB

As every woman knows, home life is a mixture of conversations, mediations, irritations, deliberations, commiserations, frustrations, negotiations and celebrations. In other words, the life of the typical mom is incredibly varied.

Certainly, in the life of every family, there are moments of frustration and disappointment. Lots of them. But, for those who are lucky enough to live in the presence of a close-knit, caring clan, the rewards far outweigh the frustrations. That's why we must pray fervently for our family members, and that's why we must love them despite their faults.

Even on those difficult days when your to-do list is full and your nerves are frayed, you must never forget this fact: Your clan is God's gift to you. That little band of men, women, kids, and babies is a priceless treasure on temporary loan from the Father above. Give thanks to the Giver for the gift of family . . . and act accordingly.

A home is a place where we find direction.

Gigi Graham Tchividjian

A TIP FOR GUARDING YOUR HEART

If you're lucky enough to be a member of a loving, supportive family, then you owe it to yourself—and to them—to share your thoughts, your hopes, your encouragement, and your love.

WORDS OF WISDOM

Family is the we of me.

Carson McCullers

There is so much compassion and understanding that is gained when we've experienced God's grace firsthand within our own families.

Lisa Whelchel

Live in the present and make the most of your opportunities to enjoy your family and friends.

Barbara Johnson

The family: We are a strange little band of characters trudging through life sharing diseases, toothpaste, coveting one another's desserts, hiding shampoo, borrowing money, locking each other out of rooms, loving, laughing, defending, and trying to figure out the common thread that bound us all together.

Erma Bombeck

GOD'S WORDS OF WISDOM

He who brings trouble on his family will inherit only wind . . . .

Proverbs 11:29 NIV

. . . these should learn first of all to put their religion into practice by caring for their own family . . . .

1 Timothy 5:4 NIV

Every kingdom divided against itself will be ruined, and every city or household divided against itself will not stand.

Matthew 12:25 NIV

Let love and faithfulness never leave you . . . write them on the tablet of your heart.

Proverbs 3:3 NIV

SUMMING IT UP

Your family is a precious gift from above, a gift that should be treasured, nurtured, and loved.

GUARD YOUR STEPS WITH BIBLE STUDY

*All Scripture is inspired by God and is profitable for teaching,
for rebuking, for correcting, for training in righteousness,
so that the man of God may be complete,
equipped for every good work.*

2 Timothy 3:16-17 Holman CSB

God's Word will guard your heart if you read it every day. The Bible is unlike any other book. It is a roadmap for life here on earth and for life eternal. As Christians, we are called upon to study God's Holy Word, to trust its promises, to follow its commandments, and to share its Good News with the world.

As believers, we must study the Bible and meditate upon its meaning for our lives. Otherwise, we deprive ourselves of a priceless gift from our Creator. God's Holy Word is, indeed, a transforming, life-changing, one-of-a-kind treasure. And, a passing acquaintance with the Good

Book is insufficient for Christians who seek to obey God's Word and to understand His will. After all, neither man nor woman should live by bread alone . . .

Every word of God is pure:
he is a shield unto them
that put their trust in him.

Proverbs 30:5 KJV

A Tip for Guarding Your Heart

Wisdom is found in God's Word. Seek to gain God's wisdom through daily Bible readings.

WORDS OF WISDOM

Only through routine, regular exposure to God's Word can you and I draw out the nutrition needed to grow a heart of faith.

Elizabeth George

One of the greatest ways God changes me is by bringing Scripture to mind that I have hidden deep in my heart. And, He always picks the right Scripture at the right time.

Evelyn Christianson

Weave the unveiling fabric of God's word through your heart and mind. It will hold strong, even if the rest of life unravels.

Gigi Graham Tchividjian

God's Word is not merely letters on paper . . . it's alive. Believe and draw near, for it longs to dance in your heart and whisper to you in the night.

Lisa Bevere

God can see clearly no matter how dark or foggy the night is. Trust His Word to guide you safely home.

Lisa Whelchel

GOD'S WORDS OF WISDOM

*Heaven and earth will pass away, but My words will never
pass away.*

Matthew 24:35 Holman CSB

*But the word of the Lord endures forever. And this is the word
that was preached as the gospel to you.*

1 Peter 1:25 Holman CSB

*For the word of God is living and effective and sharper than
any two-edged sword, penetrating as far as to divide soul,
spirit, joints, and marrow; it is a judge of the ideas and
thoughts of the heart.*

Hebrews 4:12 Holman CSB

*The one who is from God listens to God's words. This is why
you don't listen, because you are not from God.*

John 8:47 Holman CSB

SUMMING IT UP

God's Word can guide your steps and guard your heart.
Let your Bible be your guide.

GUARD YOUR STEPS AGAINST PEER PRESSURE

Dear friend, don't let this bad example influence you. Follow only what is good. Remember that those who do good prove that they are God's children, and those who do evil prove that they do not know God.

3 John 1:11 NLT

Whom will you try to please today? Your primary obligation, of course, is please your Father in heaven, not your friends in the neighborhood. But even if you're a devoted Christian, you may, from time to time, feel the urge to impress your peers—and sometimes that urge can be strong.

Peer pressure can be a good thing or a bad thing, depending upon your peers. If your peers encourage you to follow God's will and to obey His commandments, then you'll experience positive peer pressure, and that's good. But, if you are involved with friends who encourage you to do foolish things, you're facing a different kind of peer pressure . . . and you'd better beware. When you feel pressured to do things—or to say things—that lead you away from God, you're aiming straight for trouble. So don't do the "easy" thing or the "popular" thing. Do the right thing, and don't worry about winning popularity contests. Here are a few things to remember about peer pressure:

1. Peer pressure exists, and you may experience it at any age. 2. If your peers encourage you to behave yourself, to honor God, and to become a better person, peer pressure can actually be a good thing . . . up to a point. But remember: You don't have to be perfect to be wonderful. So if you're trying to be perfect, lighten up on yourself, and while you're at it, lighten up on others, too. 3. If your friends are encouraging you to misbehave or underachieve, find new friends. Today.

Rick Warren correctly observed, "Those who follow the crowd usually get lost in it." Are you satisfied to follow that crowd? If so, you will probably pay a heavy price for your shortsightedness. But if you're determined to follow the One from Galilee, He will guide your steps and bless your undertakings. To sum it up, here's your choice: You can choose to please God first, or you can fall prey to peer pressure. The choice is yours—and so are the consequences.

WORDS OF WISDOM

For better or worse, you will eventually become more and more like the people you associate with. So why not associate with people who make you better, not worse?

Marie T. Freeman

We, as God's people, are not only to stay far away from sin and sinners who would entice us, but we are to be so like our God that we mourn over sin.

Kay Arthur

You will get untold flak for prioritizing God's revealed and present will for your life over man's . . . but, boy, is it worth it.

Beth Moore

Not everybody is healthy enough to have a front-row seat in your life.

Susan L. Taylor

A TIP FOR GUARDING YOUR HEART

A thoughtful Christian doesn't follow the crowd . . . a thoughtful Christian follows Jesus.

GOD'S WORDS OF WISDOM

Do not be misled: "Bad company corrupts good character."

1 Corinthians 15:33 NIV

Don't become partners with those who reject God. How can you make a partnership out of right and wrong? That's not partnership; that's war. Is light best friends with dark?

2 Corinthians 6:14 MSG

We must obey God rather than men.

Acts 5:29 Holman CSB

Blessed is the man who walks not in the counsel of the ungodly, nor stands in the path of sinners, nor sits in the seat of the scornful; but his delight is in the law of the Lord, and in His law he meditates day and night.

Psalm 1:1-2 NKJV

SUMMING IT UP

A great way to guard your steps is by associating with friends who guard theirs.

GUARD YOUR STEPS WITH GODLY FRIENDS

As iron sharpens iron, a friend sharpens a friend.

Proverbs 27:17 NLT

Some friendships help us guard our hearts; these friendships should be nurtured. Other friendships place us in situations where we are tempted to dishonor God by disobeying His commandments; friendships such as these have the potential to do us great harm.

Because we tend to become like our friends, we must choose our friends carefully. Because our friends influence us in ways that are both subtle and powerful, we must ensure that our friendships are pleasing to God. When we spend our days in the presence of godly believers, we are blessed, not only by those friends, but also by our Creator.

Are you hanging out with people who make you a better Christian, or are you spending time with people who encourage you to stray from your faith? The answer to this question will have a surprising impact on the condition of your spiritual health. Why? Because peer pressure is very real and very powerful. So, one of the best ways to ensure that you follow Christ is to find fellow believers who are willing to follow Him with you.

Many elements of society seek to mold you into a more worldly being; God, on the other hand, seeks to mold you into a new being, a new creation through Christ, a being that is most certainly not conformed to this world. If you are to please God, you must resist the pressures that society seeks to impose upon you, and you must choose, instead, to follow in the footsteps of His only begotten Son.

I thank my God upon every remembrance of you.

Philippians 1:3 NKJV

A TIP FOR GUARDING YOUR HEART

Today, as you think about the nature and the quality of your friendships, remember the first rule of making (and keeping) friends: it's the Golden Rule, and it starts like this: "Do unto others . . . ."

WORDS OF WISDOM

Friendships are living organisms at work. They continue to unfold, change, and emerge.

Barbara Johnson

The glory of friendship is not the outstretched hand, or the kindly smile, or the joy of companionship. It is the spiritual inspiration that comes to one when he discovers that someone else believes in him and is willing to trust him with his friendship.

Corrie ten Boom

In friendship, God opens your eyes to the glories of Himself.

Joni Eareckson Tada

My special friends, who know me so well and love me anyway, give me daily encouragement to keep on.

Emilie Barnes

Friendship is the garden of God; what a delight to tend his planting!

Inez Bell Ley

GOD'S WORDS OF WISDOM

Greater love has no one than this, that he lay down his life for his friends.

John 15:13 NIV

A friend loves you all the time, and a brother helps in time of trouble.

Proverbs 17:17 NCV

If a fellow believer hurts you, go and tell him—work it out between the two of you. If he listens, you've made a friend.

Matthew 18:15 MSG

Beloved, if God so loved us, we also ought to love one another.

1 John 4:11 NKJV

SUMMING IT UP

Thank your Creator God for the godly friends He has placed along your path. Cherish those friendships, and do your best to make them flourish.

GUARD YOUR STEPS BY USING GOD'S GIFTS

Do not neglect the gift that is in you.

1 Timothy 4:14 Holman CSB

God has given you an array of talents, and He has given you unique opportunities to share those talents with the world. Your Creator intends for you to use your talents for the glory of His kingdom in the service of His children. Will you honor Him by sharing His gifts? And, will you share His gifts humbly and lovingly? Hopefully you will.

The old saying is both familiar and true: "What you are is God's gift to you; what you become is your gift to God." As a woman who has been touched by the transforming love of Jesus Christ, your obligation is clear: You must strive to make the most of your own God-given talents, and you must encourage your family and friends to do likewise.

Today, make this promise to yourself and to God: Promise to use your talents to minister to your family, to your friends, and to the world. And remember: The best way to say "Thank You" for God's gifts is to use them.

I remind you to fan into flame the gift of God.

2 Timothy 1:6 NIV

A TIP FOR GUARDING YOUR HEART

You are the sole owner of your own set of talents and opportunities. God has given you your own particular gifts—the rest is up to you.

WORDS OF WISDOM

Not everyone possesses boundless energy or a conspicuous talent. We are not equally blessed with great intellect or physical beauty or emotional strength. But we have all been given the same ability to be faithful.

Gigi Graham Tchividjian

The Lord has abundantly blessed me all of my life. I'm not trying to pay Him back for all of His wonderful gifts; I just realize that He gave them to me to give away.

Lisa Whelchel

It is the definition of joy to be able to offer back to God the essence of what he's placed in you, be that creativity or a love of ideas or a compassionate heart or the gift of hospitality.

Paula Rinehart

The splendor of the rose and the whiteness of the lily do not rob the little violet of its scent nor the daisy of its simple charm. If every tiny flower wanted to be a rose, spring would lose its loveliness.

Therese of Lisieux

GOD'S WORDS OF WISDOM

God has given gifts to each of you from his great variety of spiritual gifts. Manage them well so that God's generosity can flow through you.

1 Peter 4:10 NLT

There are different kinds of gifts, but they are all from the same Spirit. There are different ways to serve but the same Lord to serve.

1 Corinthians 12:4–5 NCV

The man who had received the five talents brought the other five. "Master," he said, "you entrusted me with five talents. See, I have gained five more." His master replied, "Well done, good and faithful servant! You have been faithful with a few things; I will put you in charge of many things. Come and share your master's happiness."

Matthew 25:20-21 NIV

SUMMING IT UP

God has given you a unique array of talents and opportunities. The rest is up to you.

GUARD YOUR STEPS
WITH WISDOM

How much better to get wisdom than gold!
And to get understanding is to be chosen rather than silver.

Proverbs 16:16 NKJV

When you obtain wisdom—and when you apply that wisdom to challenges of everyday living—you will guard your heart and you will enrich your life. But be forewarned: The acquisition of wisdom is seldom easy or quick.

Wisdom is not like a mushroom; it does not spring up overnight. It is, instead, like an oak tree that starts as a tiny acorn, grows into a sapling, and eventually reaches up to the sky, tall and strong.

Do you seek wisdom? Then seek it every day of your life. Seek it with consistency and purpose. And, seek it in the right place. That place, of course, is, first and foremost, the Word of God.

Sometimes, amid the demands of daily life, you will lose perspective. Life may seem out of balance, and the pressures of everyday living may seem overwhelming. What's needed is a fresh perspective, a restored sense of balance . . . and God's wisdom. If you call upon the Lord and seek to see the world through His eyes, He will give you guidance and perspective. If you make God's priorities your priorities, He will lead you along a path of His choosing. If you study God's teachings, you will be reminded that God's reality is the ultimate reality.

As you accumulate wisdom, you may feel the need to share your insights with friends and family members. If so, remember this: Your actions must reflect the values that you hold dear. The best way to share your wisdom—perhaps the only way—is not by your words, but by your example.

A TIP FOR GUARDING YOUR HEART

Simply put, wisdom starts with God. If you don't have God's wisdom—and if you don't live according to God's rules—you'll pay a big price later.

WORDS OF WISDOM

If we neglect the Bible, we cannot expect to benefit from the wisdom and direction that result from knowing God's Word.

Vonette Bright

Knowledge can be found in books or in school. Wisdom, on the other hand, starts with God . . . and ends there.

Marie T. Freeman

This is my song through endless ages: Jesus led me all the way.

Fanny Crosby

Wisdom is knowledge applied. Head knowledge is useless on the battlefield. Knowledge stamped on the heart makes one wise.

Beth Moore

When you and I are related to Jesus Christ, our strength and wisdom and peace and joy and love and hope may run out, but His life rushes in to keep us filled to the brim. We are showered with blessings, not because of anything we have or have not done, but simply because of Him.

Anne Graham Lotz

GOD'S WORDS OF WISDOM

The Lord says, "I will make you wise and show you where to go. I will guide you and watch over you."

Psalm 32:8 NCV

Wisdom is the principal thing; therefore get wisdom. And in all your getting, get understanding.

Proverbs 4:7 NKJV

Anyone who listens to my teaching and obeys me is wise, like a person who builds a house on solid rock. Though the rain comes in torrents and the floodwaters rise and the winds beat against that house, it won't collapse, because it is built on rock.

Matthew 7:24–25 NLT

But the wisdom that is from above is first pure, then peaceable, gentle, willing to yield, full of mercy and good fruits, without partiality and without hypocrisy.

James 3:17 NKJV

SUMMING IT UP

God makes His wisdom available to you. Your job is to acknowledge, to understand, and (above all) to use that wisdom.

GUARD YOUR STEPS
ONE DAY AT A TIME

Encourage one another daily, as long as it is Today . . . .

Hebrews 3:13 NIV

What do you expect from the day ahead? Are you expecting God to do wonderful things, or are you living beneath a cloud of apprehension and doubt? Do you expect God to use you in unexpected ways, or do you expect another uneventful day to pass with little fanfare? As a thoughtful believer, the answer to these questions should be obvious.

Christ came to this earth to give us abundant life and eternal salvation. Our task is to accept Christ's grace with joy in our hearts and praise on our lips. When we fashion our days around Jesus, we are transformed: We see the world differently, we act differently, and we feel differently about ourselves and our neighbors.

If you're a thoughtful Christian, then you're a thankful Christian. And because of your faith, you can face the inevitable challenges and disappointments of each day armed with the joy of Christ and the promise of salvation.

So whatever this day holds for you, begin it and end it with God as your partner and Christ as your Savior. And throughout the day, give thanks to the One who created you and saved you. God's love for you is infinite—accept it joyfully and be thankful.

This is the day which the LORD has made;
let us rejoice and be glad in it.

Psalm 118:24 NASB

A TIP FOR GUARDING YOUR HEART

Take time to celebrate another day of life. And while you're at it, encourage your family and friends to join in the celebration.

WORDS OF WISDOM

Live today fully, expressing gratitude for all you have been, all you are right now, and all you are becoming.

Melodie Beattie

Every day of our lives we make choices about how we're going to live that day.

Luci Swindoll

Submit each day to God, knowing that He is God over all your tomorrows.

Kay Arthur

Lovely, complicated wrappings sheath the gift of one-day-more; breathless, I untie the package—never lived this day before!

Gloria Gaither

Today is mine. Tomorrow is none of my business. If I peer anxiously into the fog of the future, I will strain my spiritual eyes so that I will not see clearly what is required of me now.

Elisabeth Elliot

GOD'S WORDS OF WISDOM

For he says, "In the time of my favor I heard you, and in the day of salvation I helped you." I tell you, now is the time of God's favor, now is the day of salvation.

2 Corinthians 6:2 NIV

Give your entire attention to what God is doing right now, and don't get worked up about what may or may not happen tomorrow. God will help you deal with whatever hard things come up when the time comes.

Matthew 6:34 MSG

While it is daytime, we must continue doing the work of the One who sent me. Night is coming, when no one can work.

John 9:4 NCV

SUMMING IT UP

Today is a wonderful, one-of-a-kind gift from God. Treat it that way.

GUARD YOUR STEPS WITH FELLOWSHIP

You must get along with each other.
You must learn to be considerate of one another,
cultivating a life in common.

1 Corinthians 1:10 MSG

You can guard your steps by associating yourself with a faithful group of fellow believers—and you should. Your association with fellow Christians should be uplifting, enlightening, encouraging, and consistent. In short, fellowship with other believers should be an integral part of your everyday life.

Are you an active member of your own fellowship? Are you a builder of bridges inside the four walls of your church and outside it? Do you contribute to God's glory by contributing your time and your talents to a close-knit band of believers? Hopefully so. The fellowship of believers is intended to be a powerful tool for spreading

God's Good News and uplifting His children. And God intends for you to be a fully contributing member of that fellowship. Your intentions should be the same.

*Don't you realize that all of you together
are the temple of God
and that the Spirit of God lives in you?*

1 Corinthians 3:16 NLT

A TIP FOR GUARDING YOUR HEART

Christians are not Lone Rangers. They are members of a spiritual family, and they need one another.

WORDS OF WISDOM

Be united with other Christians. A wall with loose bricks is not good. The bricks must be cemented together.

Corrie ten Boom

Only when we realize that we are indeed broken, that we are not independent, that we cannot do it ourselves, can we turn to God and take that which he has given us, no matter what it is, and create with it.

Madeleine L'Engle

In God's economy you will be hard-pressed to find many examples of successful "Lone Rangers."

Luci Swindoll

It is wonderful to have all kinds of human support systems, but we must always stand firm in God and in Him alone.

Joyce Meyer

One of the ways God refills us after failure is through the blessing of Christian fellowship. Just experiencing the joy of simple activities shared with other children of God can have a healing effect on us.

Anne Graham Lotz

GOD'S WORDS OF WISDOM

He keeps us in step with each other. His very breath and blood flow through us, nourishing us so that we will grow up healthy in God, robust in love.

Ephesians 4:16 MSG

You can develop a healthy, robust community that lives right with God and enjoy its results only if you do the hard work of getting along with each other, treating each other with dignity and honor.

James 3:18 MSG

To turn from evil is understanding.

Job 28:28 Holman CSB

SUMMING IT UP

You need fellowship with men and women of faith. And your Christian friends need fellowship with you. So what are you waiting for?

GUARD YOUR STEPS BY WALKING IN CHRIST'S FOOTSTEPS

"Follow Me," Jesus told them, "and I will make you into fishers of men!" Immediately they left their nets and followed Him.

Mark 1:17-18 Holman CSB

When Jesus addressed His disciples, He warned that each one must "take up his cross and follow me." The disciples must have known exactly what the Master meant. In Jesus' day, prisoners were forced to carry their own crosses to the location where they would be put to death. Thus, Christ's message was clear: In order to follow Him, Christ's disciples must deny themselves and, instead, trust Him completely. Nothing has changed since then.

If we are to be disciples of Christ, we must trust Him and place Him at the very center of our beings. Jesus never comes "next." He is always first. The paradox, of course, is that only by sacrificing ourselves to Him do we gain salvation for ourselves.

Do you seek to be a worthy disciple of Christ? Then pick up His cross today and every day that you live. When you do, He will bless you now and forever.

If we just give God the little that we have,
we can trust Him to make it go around.

Gloria Gaither

A TIP FOR GUARDING YOUR HEART

Today, think of at least one single step that you can take to become a better disciple for Christ. Then, take that step.

WORDS OF WISDOM

When Jesus put the little child in the midst of His disciples, He did not tell the little child to become like His disciples; He told the disciples to become like the little child.

Ruth Bell Graham

You cannot cooperate with Jesus in becoming what He wants you to become and simultaneously be what the world desires to make you. If you would say, "Take the world but give me Jesus," then you must deny yourself and take up your cross. The simple truth is that your "self" must be put to death in order for you to get to the point where for you to live is Christ. What will it be? The world and you, or Jesus and you? You do have a choice to make.

Kay Arthur

Discipleship usually brings us into the necessity of choice between duty and desire.

Elisabeth Elliot

GOD'S WORDS OF WISDOM

Be imitators of God, therefore, as dearly loved children.

Ephesians 5:1 NIV

Work hard, but not just to please your masters when they are watching. As slaves of Christ, do the will of God with all your heart. Work with enthusiasm, as though you were working for the Lord rather than for people.

Ephesians 6:6-7 NLT

Then Jesus said to His disciples, "If anyone wants to come with Me, he must deny himself, take up his cross, and follow Me.

Matthew 16:24 Holman CSB

All of us who look forward to his Coming stay ready, with the glistening purity of Jesus' life as a model for our own.

1 John 3:3 MSG

SUMMING IT UP

Jesus has invited you to become His disciple. If you accept His invitation—and if you obey His commandments—you will be protected and blessed.

PART 4

GUARD
YOUR HEART

*Above all else, guard your heart, for it affects
everything you do. Avoid all perverse talk;
stay far from corrupt speech. Look straight ahead,
and fix your eyes on what lies before you.
Mark out a straight path for your feet; then stick
to the path and stay safe. Don't get sidetracked;
keep your feet from following evil.*

Proverbs 4:23 NLT

JESUS' PRINCIPLES OF PRAYER

*And when you pray, do not be like the hypocrites, for they
love to pray standing in the synagogues and on the street
corners to be seen by men. I tell you the truth, they have
received their reward in full. But when you pray, go into your
room, close the door and pray to your Father, who is unseen.
Then your Father, who sees what is done in secret, will reward
you. And when you pray, do not keep on babbling like pagans,
for they think they will be heard because of their many words.
Do not be like them, for your Father knows
what you need before you ask him.*

Matthew 6:5-8 NIV

If you sincerely wish to guard your heart, no discipline
is more important than the discipline of prayer. In the
sixth chapter of Matthew, Jesus offers the Bible's first
extensive instructions regarding prayer. It is here that Jesus
offers five principles about prayer that still apply.

Principle #1: Pray Regularly. Jesus began His lesson on prayer with the words, "And when you pray . . . " He did not say "if you pray." Prayer was assumed to be a regular daily activity for Christians. In truth, the Christian life cannot be maintained without consistent daily prayer.

Many Christians talk about their "prayer life." Yet God is not as interested in our having "prayer lives" as He is in our having "lives of prayer." And make no mistake: there's a big difference. A "prayer life" indicates that we divide our daily activities into times of prayer and times of non-prayer. What God prefers is that the entirety of a Christian's life should become a constant prayer lifted to Him—every activity dedicated to Him, every part of the day an act of worship.

Principle #2: Pray Privately. Jesus teaches that our times of protracted, concentrated prayer are not to be public spectacles, but are to be private. He admonishes us to go into our rooms, to close the door, and to talk to our Father who is unseen.

Does this mean that we are to never pray publicly? No, but it does mean that most of our prayers are to be private communications, just between God and us.

Some folks may say, "Well, I pray with my family." And, of course, that's an admirable activity. Others may say, "I am in a prayer group at church." And once again, God will be pleased. But nothing should obscure the fact that the majority of our concentrated prayer times are to be private.

Principle #3: Have a Time and Place for Prayer. What we schedule, we do. What we don't schedule, we may never get around to doing. So it's best to set aside a specific time for concentrated prayer.

Jesus had a set time of concentrated prayer—the early morning. Not a morning person? Then try the evening, or maybe during your lunch break. But whatever you do, have a regular, daily time of prayer . . . and have a place.

Jesus prayed outdoors; maybe you find that too distracting. If so, find a room where you can shut the door and pray. Do whatever works for you, but make certain that you have a specific place and time each day when you do nothing, absolutely nothing, but talk to the Father.

Principle #4: Prayer Is Rewarded. We sometimes baulk at the idea that we will be rewarded for doing what we consider to be our duty. Yet if Jesus did not want us to know about the rewards of prayer, He would not have told us that "your Father, who sees what is done in secret, will reward you" (Matthew 6:6).

Do these rewards come now or later? Of course, there may be many earthly rewards for prayer; and we most assuredly benefit from the blessings that arise from the act of praying. But we can also be certain that our prayers will be rewarded in heaven.

Principle #5: Keep It Simple. Jesus said that we are not to pray, "babbling like pagans, for they think they will be heard because of their many words." He tells us that our Father knows what we need before we ask Him. So, we can keep our prayers short, sweet, and simple. We needn't try to impress God by fancy speeches or lengthy lectures. God isn't concerned with the eloquence of our words, which, by the way, is a very good thing. That means that all of us can talk intimately with God . . . and He always understands.

I want men everywhere to lift up holy hands
in prayer, without anger or disputing.

1 Timothy 2:8 NIV

A TIP FOR GUARDING YOUR HEART

Pray early and often. One way to make sure that your heart is in tune with God is to pray often. The more you talk to God, the more He will talk to you.

WORDS OF WISDOM

What God gives in answer to our prayers will always be the thing we most urgently need, and it will always be sufficient.

Elisabeth Elliot

Your family and friends need your prayers and you need theirs. And God wants to hear those prayers. So what are you waiting for?

Marie T. Freeman

God says we don't need to be anxious about anything; we just need to pray about everything.

Stormie Omartian

When the Holy Spirit comes to dwell within us, I believe we gain a built-in inclination to take our concerns and needs to the Lord in prayer.

Shirley Dobson

The center of power is not to be found in summit meetings or in peace conferences. It is not in Peking or Washington or the United Nations, but rather where a child of God prays in the power of the Spirit for God's will to be done in her life, in her home, and in the world around her.

Ruth Bell Graham

GOD'S WORDS OF WISDOM

*"Relax, Daniel," he continued, "don't be afraid. From
the moment you decided to humble yourself to receive
understanding, your prayer was heard, and I set out to come to
you."*

Daniel 10:12 MSG

*If my people who are called by my name, will humble
themselves and pray and seek my face and turn from their
wicked ways, then will I hear from heaven and will forgive their
sin and will heal their land.*

2 Chronicles 7:14 NIV

*Ask and it shall be given to you; seek and you shall find; knock
and it shall be opened to you. For every one who asks receives,
and he who seeks finds, and to him who knocks it shall be
opened.*

Matthew 7:7-8 NASB

SUMMING IT UP

Prayer changes things—and you—so pray.

ABOVE ALL ELSE
GUARD YOUR HEART

Above all else, guard your heart,
for it affects everything you do.

Proverbs 4:23 NLT

Life is a series of choices. Each day, we make countless decisions that can bring us closer to God . . . or not. When we live according to God's commandments, we earn for ourselves the abundance and peace that He intends for us to experience. But, when we turn our backs upon God by disobeying Him, we bring needless suffering upon ourselves and our families.

Do you seek God's peace and His blessings? Then obey Him. When you're faced with a difficult choice or a powerful temptation, seek God's counsel and trust the counsel He gives. Invite God into your heart and live according to His commandments. When you do, you will be blessed today, tomorrow, and forever.

God has given you a guidebook for righteous living called the Holy Bible. It contains thorough instructions which, if followed, lead to protection, fulfillment, and salvation. But, if you choose to ignore God's commandments, the results are as predictable as they are tragic.

So here's a surefire formula for a happy, abundant life: live righteously.

And for further instructions, read the manual.

> *Blessed are the pure of heart,*
> *for they will see God.*
>
> Matthew 5:8 NIV

A TIP FOR GUARDING YOUR HEART

Today, consider the value of living a life that is pleasing to God. And while you're at it, think about the rewards that are likely to be yours when you do the right thing day in and day out.

WORDS OF WISDOM

Our afflictions are designed not to break us but to bend us toward the eternal and the holy.

Barbara Johnson

Becoming pure is a process of spiritual growth, and taking seriously the confession of sin during prayer time moves that process along, causing us to purge our life of practices that displease God.

Elizabeth George

Holiness has never been the driving force of the majority. It is, however, mandatory for anyone who wants to enter the kingdom.

Elisabeth Elliot

He doesn't need an abundance of words. He doesn't need a dissertation about your life. He just wants your attention. He wants your heart.

Kathy Troccoli

Holiness is not God's asking us to be "good"; it is an invitation to be "His."

Lisa Bevere

GOD'S WORDS OF WISDOM

For the eyes of the Lord are over the righteous, and his ears are open unto their prayers: but the face of the Lord is against them that do evil.

1 Peter 3:12 KJV

But seek first his kingdom and his righteousness, and all these things will be given to you as well.

Matthew 6:33 NIV

The Lord will not reject his people; he will not abandon his own special possession. Judgement will come again for the righteous, and those who are upright will have a reward.

Psalm 94:14-15 NLT

The righteous shall flourish like the palm tree: he shall grow like a cedar in Lebanon.

Psalm 92:12 KJV

SUMMING IT UP

Because God is just, He rewards righteousness just as surely as He punishes sin.

GUARD YOUR HEART WITH GOD'S PROMISES

God also bound himself with an oath, so that those who received the promise could be perfectly sure that he would never change his mind. So God has given us both his promise and his oath. These two things are unchangeable because it is impossible for God to lie. Therefore, we who have fled to him for refuge can take new courage, for we can hold on to his promise with confidence.

Hebrews 6:17-18 NLT

You can guard your heart by standing on the promises of God. And that's precisely what you should do.

What do you expect from the day ahead? Are you willing to trust God completely or are you living beneath a cloud of doubt and fear? God's Word makes it clear: You should trust Him and His promises, and when you do, you can live courageously.

For thoughtful Christians, every day begins and ends with God's Son and God's promises. When we accept Christ into our hearts, God promises us the opportunity for earthy peace and spiritual abundance. But more importantly, God promises us the priceless gift of eternal life.

Sometimes, especially when we find ourselves caught in the inevitable entanglements of life, we fail to trust God completely.

Are you tired? Discouraged? Fearful? Be comforted and trust the promises that God has made to you. Are you worried or anxious? Be confident in God's power. Do you see a difficult future ahead? Be courageous and call upon God. He will protect you and then use you according to His purposes. Are you confused? Listen to the quiet voice of your Heavenly Father. He is not a God of confusion. Talk with Him; listen to Him; trust Him, and trust His promises. He is steadfast, and He is your Protector . . . forever.

A TIP FOR GUARDING YOUR HEART

Do you really trust God's promises, or are you hedging your bets? Today, think about the role that God's Word plays in your life, and think about ways that you can worry less and trust God more.

WORDS OF WISDOM

Joy is not mere happiness. Nor does joy spring from a life of ease, comfort, or peaceful circumstances. Joy is the soul's buoyant response to a God of promise, presence, and power.

Susan Lenzkes

The meaning of hope isn't just some flimsy wishing. It's a firm confidence in God's promises—that he will ultimately set things right.

Sheila Walsh

In Biblical worship you do not find the repetition of a phrase; instead, you find the worshipers rehearsing the character of God and His ways, reminding Him of His faithfulness and His wonderful promises.

Kay Arthur

Gather the riches of God's promises which can strengthen you in the time when there will be no freedom.

Corrie ten Boom

No giant will ever be a match for a big God with a little rock.

Beth Moore

GOD'S WORDS OF WISDOM

Whatever God has promised gets stamped with the Yes of Jesus.
In him, this is what we preach and pray, the great Amen,
God's Yes and our Yes together, gloriously evident.

2 Corinthians 1:20 MSG

Let us hold on to the confession of our hope without wavering,
for He who promised is faithful.

Hebrews 10:23 Holman CSB

Patient endurance is what you need now, so you will continue
to do God's will. Then you will receive all that he has
promised.

Hebrews 10:36 NLT

As for God, his way is perfect. All the Lord's promises prove
true. He is a shield for all who look to him for protection.

Psalm 18:30 NLT

SUMMING IT UP

God will most certainly keep His promises to you. Your
job is to keep your obligations to Him.

GUARD YOUR HEART WITH MOUNTAIN-MOVING FAITH

For truly I say to you, if you have faith as a mustard seed,
you shall say to this mountain,
"Move from here to there" and it shall move;
and nothing shall be impossible to you.

Matthew 17:20 NASB

A suffering woman sought healing in an unusual way: she simply touched the hem of Jesus' garment. When she did, Jesus turned and said, "Daughter, be of good comfort; thy faith hath made thee whole" (Matthew 9:22 KJV). We, too, can be made whole when we place our faith completely and unwaveringly in the person of Jesus Christ.

Concentration camp survivor Corrie ten Boom relied on faith during ten months of imprisonment and torture. Later, despite the fact that four of her family members had died in Nazi death camps, Corrie's faith was unshaken. She wrote, "There is no pit so deep that God's love is not deeper still." Christians take note: Genuine faith in God means faith in all circumstances, happy or sad, joyful or tragic.

When you place your faith, your trust, indeed your life in the hands of Christ Jesus, you'll be amazed at the marvelous things He can do with you and through you. So strengthen your faith through praise, through worship, through Bible study, and through prayer. Then, trust God's plans. Your Heavenly Father is standing at the door of your heart. If you reach out to Him in faith, He will give you peace and heal your broken spirit. Be content to touch even the smallest fragment of the Master's garment, and He will make you whole.

A TIP FOR GUARDING YOUR HEART

If you don't have faith, you'll never move mountains. But if you do have faith, there's no limit to the things that you and God, working together, can accomplish.

WORDS OF WISDOM

Faith is seeing light with the eyes of your heart, when the eyes of your body see only darkness.

Barbara Johnson

Joy is faith feasting and celebrating the One in Whom it trusts.

Susan Lenzkes

Just as our faith strengthens our prayer life, so do our prayers deepen our faith. Let us pray often, starting today, for a deeper, more powerful faith.

Shirley Dobson

I want my life to be a faith-filled leap into his arms, knowing he will be there—not that everything will go as I want, but that he will be there and that this will be enough.

Sheila Walsh

If God chooses to remain silent, faith is content.

Ruth Bell Graham

GOD'S WORDS OF WISDOM

For whatever is born of God overcomes the world. And this is the victory that has overcome the world—our faith.

1 John 5:4 NKJV

It is impossible to please God apart from faith. And why? Because anyone who wants to approach God must believe both that he exists and that he cares enough to respond to those who seek him.

Hebrews 11:6 MSG

Fight the good fight of faith; take hold of the eternal life to which you were called . . . .

1 Timothy 6:12 NASB

Have faith in the Lord your God and you will be upheld . . . .

2 Chronicles 20:20 NIV

SUMMING IT UP

If your faith is strong enough, you and God—working together—can move mountains.

GUARD YOUR HEART AGAINST DISCONTENTMENT

I have learned to be content whatever the circumstances.

Philippians 4:11 NIV

Everywhere we turn, or so it seems, the world promises us contentment and happiness. We are bombarded by messages offering us the "good life" if only we will purchase products and services that are designed to provide happiness, success, and contentment. But the contentment that the world offers is fleeting and incomplete. Thankfully, the contentment that God offers is all encompassing and everlasting.

Happiness depends less upon our circumstances than upon our thoughts. When we turn our thoughts to God, to His gifts, and to His glorious creation, we experience the joy that God intends for His children. But, when we focus on the negative aspects of life—or when we disobey God's commandments—we cause ourselves needless suffering.

Do you sincerely want to be a contented Christian? Then set your mind and your heart upon God's love and His grace. Seek first the salvation that is available through a personal relationship with Jesus Christ, and then claim the joy, the contentment, and the spiritual abundance that God offers His children.

A tranquil heart is life to the body,
but jealousy is rottenness to the bones.

Proverbs 14:30 Holman CSB

A TIP FOR GUARDING YOUR HEART

Contentment comes, not from your circumstances, but from your attitude. And remember this: Peace with God is the foundation of a contented life.

WORDS OF WISDOM

We will never be happy until we make God the source of our fulfillment and the answer to our longings.

Stormie Omartian

If I could just hang in there, being faithful to my own tasks, God would make me joyful and content. The responsibility is mine, but the power is His.

Peg Rankin

The key to contentment is to consider. Consider who you are and be satisfied with that. Consider what you have and be satisfied with that. Consider what God's doing and be satisfied with that.

Luci Swindoll

When we are set free from the bondage of pleasing others, when we are free from currying others' favor and others' approval—then no one will be able to make us miserable or dissatisfied. And then, if we know we have pleased God, contentment will be our consolation.

Kay Arthur

Those who are God's without reserve are, in every sense, content.

Hannah Whitall Smith

GOD'S WORDS OF WISDOM

But godliness with contentment is great gain. For we brought nothing into the world, and we can take nothing out of it. But if we have food and clothing, we will be content with that.

1 Timothy 6:6-8 NIV

Let your character be free from the love of money, being content with what you have; for He Himself has said, "I will never desert you, nor will I ever forsake you."

Hebrews 13:5 NASB

Because your love is better than life, my lips will glorify you. I will praise you as long as I live, and in your name I will lift up my hands. My soul will be satisfied as with the richest of foods; with singing lips my mouth will praise you.

Psalm 63:3-5 NIV

SUMMING IT UP

God offers you His peace, His protection, and His promises. If you accept these gifts, you will be content.

GUARD YOUR HEART AGAINST DOUBTS

When doubts filled my mind,
your comfort gave me renewed hope and cheer.

Psalm 94:19 NLT

Have you ever felt your faith in God slipping away? If so, you are not alone. Every life—including yours—is a series of successes and failures, celebrations and disappointments, joys and sorrows, hopes and doubts. Even the most faithful Christians are overcome by occasional bouts of fear and doubt, and so, too, will you.

Doubts come in several shapes and sizes: doubts about God, doubts about the future, and doubts about your own abilities, for starters. And what, precisely, does God's Word say in response to these doubts? The Bible is clear: When we are beset by doubts, of whatever kind, we must guard our hearts as we draw ourselves nearer to God through worship and through prayer. When we do so,

God, the loving Father who has never left our sides, draws ever closer to us (James 4:8).

Will your faith be tested from time to time? Of course it will be. And will you have doubts about God's willingness to fulfill His promises? Perhaps you will. But even when you feel far removed from God, God never leaves your side, not for an instant. He is always with you, always willing to calm the storms of life. When you sincerely seek His presence—and when you genuinely seek to establish a deeper, more meaningful relationship with His Son—God is prepared to touch your heart, to calm your fears, to answer your doubts, and to restore your soul.

Purify your hearts, ye double-minded.

James 4:8 KJV

A TIP FOR GUARDING YOUR HEART

Are you sincerely looking for a way to address your doubts? Try Bible study, prayer, and worship.

WORDS OF WISDOM

Unconfessed sin in your life will cause you to doubt.

Anne Graham Lotz

Just as I am, though tossed about with many a conflict, many a doubt, fightings and fears within, without, / O Lamb of God, I come, I come.

Charlotte Elliott

I was learning something important: we are most vulnerable to the piercing winds of doubt when we distance ourselves from the mission and fellowship to which Christ has called us. Our night of discouragement will seem endless and our task impossible, unless we recognize that He stands in our midst.

Joni Eareckson Tada

To wrestle with God does not mean that we have lost faith, but that we are fighting for it.

Sheila Walsh

Fear and doubt are conquered by a faith that rejoices. And faith can rejoice because the promises of God are as certain as God Himself.

Kay Arthur

GOD'S WORDS OF WISDOM

Immediately the father of the boy cried out, "I do believe! Help my unbelief."

Mark 9:24 Holman CSB

Come! He said. And climbing out of the boat, Peter started walking on the water and came toward Jesus. But when he saw the strength of the wind, he was afraid. And beginning to sink he cried out, "Lord, save me!" Immediately Jesus reached out His hand, caught hold of him, and said to him, "You of little faith, why did you doubt?" When they got into the boat, the wind ceased.

Matthew 14:29-32 Holman CSB

Jesus said, "Because you have seen Me, you have believed. Blessed are those who believe without seeing."

John 20:29 Holman CSB

SUMMING IT UP

When you have fears or doubts, don't ignore them. Talk to family, to friends, and, most importantly, to God.

GUARD YOUR HEART BY COUNTING YOUR BLESSINGS

Blessings are on the head of the righteous.

Proverbs 10:6 Holman CSB

Have you counted your blessings lately? If you sincerely want to guard your heart—and if you wish to follow in Christ's footsteps—you should make thanksgiving a habit, a regular part of your daily routine.

How has God blessed you? First and foremost, He has given you the gift of eternal life through the sacrifice of His only begotten Son, but the blessings don't stop there. Today, take time to make a partial list of God's gifts to you: the talents, the opportunities, the possessions, and the relationships that you may, on occasion, take for granted. And then, when you've spent sufficient time listing your blessings, offer a prayer of gratitude to the Giver of all things good . . . and, to the best of your ability, use your gifts for the glory of His kingdom.

For surely, O Lord, you bless the righteous;
you surround them with your favor
as with a shield.

Psalm 5:12 NIV

A TIP FOR GUARDING YOUR HEART

Count your blessings . . . if you can! If you need a little cheering up, start counting your blessings. In truth, you really have too many blessings to count, but it never hurts to try.

WORDS OF WISDOM

God is always far more willing to give us good things than we are anxious to have them.

Catherine Marshall

I am convinced our hearts are not healthy until they have been satisfied by the only completely healthy love that exists: the love of God Himself.

Beth Moore

The Christian life is motivated, not by a list of do's and don'ts, but by the gracious outpouring of God's love and blessing.

Anne Graham Lotz

The unfolding of our friendship with the Father will be a never-ending revelation stretching on into eternity.

Catherine Marshall

God is a God of unconditional, unremitting love, a love that corrects and chastens but never ceases.

Kay Arthur

GOD'S WORDS OF WISDOM

You will show me the path of life; in Your presence is fullness of joy; at Your right hand are pleasures forevermore.

Psalm 16:11 NKJV

The Lord is kind and merciful, slow to get angry, full of unfailing love. The Lord is good to everyone. He showers compassion on all his creation.

Psalm 145:8-9 NLT

Blessed is a man who endures trials, because when he passes the test he will receive the crown of life that He has promised to those who love Him.

James 1:12 Holman CSB

Unfailing love surrounds those who trust the Lord.

Psalm 32:10 NLT

SUMMING IT UP

God has given you more blessings than you can count. Your job is to accept them and be grateful.

GUARD YOUR HEART BY SENSING GOD'S PRESENCE

Draw near to God, and He will draw near to you.

James 4:8 Holman CSB

If God is everywhere, why does He sometimes seem so far away? The answer to that question, of course, has nothing to do with God and everything to do with us.

When we begin each day on our knees, in praise and worship to Him, God often seems very near indeed. But, if we ignore God's presence or—worse yet—rebel against it altogether, the world in which we live becomes a spiritual wasteland.

Are you tired, discouraged, or fearful? Be comforted because God is with you. Are you confused? Listen to the quiet voice of your Heavenly Father. Are you bitter? Talk with God and seek His guidance. Are you celebrating a great victory? Thank God and praise Him. He is the Giver of all things good.

In whatever condition you find yourself, wherever you are, whether you are happy or sad, victorious or vanquished, troubled or triumphant, celebrate God's presence. And be comforted. God is not just near. He is here.

You will seek Me and find Me
when you search for Me with all your heart.

Jeremiah 29:13 Holman CSB

A TIP FOR GUARDING YOUR HEART

Having trouble hearing God? If so, slow yourself down, tune out the distractions, and listen carefully. God has important things to say; your task is to be still and listen.

WORDS OF WISDOM

What God promises is that He always, always comes. He always shows up. He always saves. He always rescues. His timing is not ours. His methods are usually unconventional. But what we can know, what we can settle in our soul, is that He is faithful to come when we call.

Angela Thomas

Through the death and broken body of Jesus Christ on the Cross, you and I have been given access to the presence of God when we approach Him by faith in prayer.

Anne Graham Lotz

God's presence is such a cleansing fire, confession and repentance are always there.

Anne Ortlund

Give yourself a gift today: be present with yourself. God is. Enjoy your own personality. God does.

Barbara Johnson

The love of God is so vast, the power of his touch so invigorating, we could just stay in his presence for hours, soaking up his glory, basking in His blessings.

Debra Evans

GOD'S WORDS OF WISDOM

No, I will not abandon you as orphans—I will come to you.

John 14:18 NLT

Again, this is God's command: to believe in his personally named Son, Jesus Christ. He told us to love each other, in line with the original command. As we keep his commands, we live deeply and surely in him, and he lives in us. And this is how we experience his deep and abiding presence in us: by the Spirit he gave us.

1 John 3:23-24 MSG

For the eyes of the Lord range throughout the earth to strengthen those whose hearts are fully committed to him.

2 Chronicles 16:9 NIV

God did this so that men would seek him and perhaps reach out for him and find him, though he is not far from each one of us.

Acts 17:27 NIV

SUMMING IT UP

God isn't far away. He's right here, right now.

GUARD YOUR HEART BY ACCEPTING GOD'S PEACE

The peace of God, which surpasses all understanding,
will guard your hearts and minds through Christ Jesus.

Philippians 4:7 NKJV

The beautiful words of John 14:27 give us hope: "Peace I leave with you, my peace I give unto you . . . ." Jesus offers us peace, not as the world gives, but as He alone gives. We, as believers, can accept His peace or ignore it.

When we accept the peace of Jesus Christ into our hearts, our lives are transformed. And then, because we possess the gift of peace, we can share that gift with fellow Christians, family members, friends, and associates. If, on the other hand, we choose to ignore the gift of peace—for whatever reason—we cannot share what we do not possess.

As every woman knows, peace can be a scarce commodity in a demanding, 21st-century world. How, then, can we find the peace that we so desperately desire? By turning our days and our lives over to God. Elisabeth Elliot writes, "If my life is surrendered to God, all is well. Let me not grab it back, as though it were in peril in His hand but would be safer in mine!" May we give our lives, our hopes, and our prayers to the Lord, and, by doing so, accept His will and His peace.

Those who love Your law have great peace,
and nothing causes them to stumble.

Psalm 119:165 NASB

A TIP FOR GUARDING YOUR HEART

God's peace can be yours right now . . . if you open up your heart and invite Him in.

WORDS OF WISDOM

Prayer guards hearts and minds and causes God to bring peace out of chaos.

Beth Moore

I want first of all . . . to be at peace with myself. I want a singleness of eye, a purity of intention, a central core to my life . . . . I want, in fact—to borrow from the language of the saints—to live "in grace" as much of the time as possible.

Anne Morrow Lindbergh

When we do what is right, we have contentment, peace, and happiness.

Beverly LaHaye

To know God as He really is—in His essential nature and character—is to arrive at a citadel of peace that circumstances may storm, but can never capture.

Catherine Marshall

In the center of a hurricane there is absolute quiet and peace. There is no safer place than in the center of the will of God.

Corrie ten Boom

GOD'S WORDS OF WISDOM

God has called us to live in peace.

1 Corinthians 7:15 NIV

And let the peace of God rule in your hearts . . . and be ye thankful.

Colossians 3:15 KJV

You will keep in perfect peace him whose mind is steadfast, because he trusts in you.

Isaiah 26:3 NIV

I have told you these things, so that in me you may have peace. In this world you will have trouble. But take heart! I have overcome the world.

John 16:33 NIV

SUMMING IT UP

God offers peace that passes human understanding . . . and He wants you to make His peace your peace.

GUARD YOUR HEART WITH LOVE

And now abide faith, hope, love, these three;
but the greatest of these is love.

1 Corinthians 13:13 NKJV

L ove is a choice. Either you choose to behave lovingly toward others . . . or not; either you behave yourself in ways that enhance your relationships . . . or not. But make no mistake: Genuine love requires effort. Simply put, if you wish to build lasting relationships, you must be willing to do your part.

Since the days of Adam and Eve, God has allowed His children to make choices for themselves, and so it is with you. As you interact with family and friends, you have choices to make . . . lots of them. If you choose wisely, you'll be rewarded; if you choose unwisely, you'll bear the consequences.

Christ's words are clear: We are to love God first, and secondly, we are to love others as we love ourselves (Matthew 22:37-40). These two commands are seldom easy, and because we are imperfect beings, we often fall short. But God's Holy Word commands us to try.

The Christian path is an exercise in love and forgiveness. If we are to walk in Christ's footsteps, we must forgive those who have done us harm, and we must accept Christ's love by sharing it freely with family, friends, neighbors, and even strangers.

God does not intend for you to experience mediocre relationships; He created you for far greater things. Building lasting relationships requires compassion, wisdom, empathy, kindness, courtesy, and forgiveness. If that sounds like work, it is—which is perfectly fine with God. Why? Because He knows that you are capable of doing that work, and because He knows that the fruits of your labors will enrich the lives of your loved ones and the lives of generations yet unborn.

A TIP FOR GUARDING YOUR HEART

Be imaginative. There are so many ways to say, "I love you." Find them. Put love notes in lunch pails and on pillows; hug relentlessly; laugh and play with abandon.

WORDS OF WISDOM

Our Lord does not care so much for the importance of our works as for the love with which they are done.

St. Teresa of Avila

Love is a fruit in season and within reach of every hand.

Mother Teresa

Love is a great beautifier.

Louisa May Alcott

Service is love in overalls!

Anonymous

Prayer is the ultimate love language. It communicates in ways we can't.

Stormie Omartian

GOD'S WORDS OF WISDOM

Though I speak with the tongues of men and of angels, but have not love, I have become sounding brass or a clanging cymbal.

1 Corinthians 13:1 NKJV

Beloved, if God so loved us, we also ought to love one another.

1 John 4:11 NASB

Love one another deeply, from the heart.

1 Peter 1:22 NIV

Above all, love each other deeply, because love covers over a multitude of sins.

1 Peter 4:8 NIV

May the Lord cause you to increase and abound in love for one another, and for all people.

1 Thessalonians 3:12 NASB

SUMMING IT UP

God is love, and He expects you to share His love with others.

GUARD YOUR HEART BY LIVING PURPOSEFULLY

You will show me the path of life;
in Your presence is fullness of joy;
at Your right hand are pleasures forevermore.

Psalm 16:11 NKJV

"What on earth does God intend for me to do with my life?" It's an easy question to ask but, for many of us, a difficult question to answer. Why? Because God's purposes aren't always clear to us. Sometimes we wander aimlessly in a wilderness of our own making. And sometimes, we struggle mightily against God in an unsuccessful attempt to find success and happiness through our own means, not His.

If you're a woman who sincerely seeks God's guidance, He will give it. But, He will make His revelations known to you in a way and in a time of His choosing, not yours, so be patient. If you prayerfully petition God and work diligently to discern His intentions, He will, in time, lead you to a place of joyful abundance and eternal peace.

Sometimes, God's intentions will be clear to you; other times, God's plan will seem uncertain at best. But even on those difficult days when you are unsure which way to turn, you must never lose sight of these overriding facts: God created you for a reason; He has important work for you to do; and He's waiting patiently for you to do it.

And the next step is up to you.

A Tip for Guarding Your Heart

Discovering God's purpose for your life requires a willingness to be open. God's plan is unfolding day by day. If you keep your eyes and your heart open, He'll reveal His plans. God has big things in store for you, but He may have quite a few lessons to teach you before you are fully prepared to do His will and fulfill His purposes.

WORDS OF WISDOM

Yesterday is just experience but tomorrow is glistening with purpose—and today is the channel leading from one to the other.

Barbara Johnson

Only God's chosen task for you will ultimately satisfy. Do not wait until it is too late to realize the privilege of serving Him in His chosen position for you.

Beth Moore

In the very place where God has put us, whatever its limitations, whatever kind of work it may be, we may indeed serve the Lord Christ.

Elisabeth Elliot

How much of our lives are, well, so daily. How often our hours are filled with the mundane, seemingly unimportant things that have to be done, whether at home or work. These very "daily" tasks could become a celebration of praise. "It is through consecration," someone has said, "that drudgery is made divine."

Gigi Graham Tchividjian

GOD'S WORDS OF WISDOM

Whatever you do, do all to the glory of God.

1 Corinthians 10:31 NKJV

You're sons of Light, daughters of Day. We live under wide open skies and know where we stand. So let's not sleepwalk through life . . .

1 Thessalonians 5:5-6 MSG

We look at this Son and see the God who cannot be seen. We look at this Son and see God's original purpose in everything created.

Colossians 1:15 MSG

There is one thing I always do. Forgetting the past and straining toward what is ahead, I keep trying to reach the goal and get the prize for which God called me . . . .

Philippians 3:13–14 NCV

SUMMING IT UP

When you gain a clear vision of your purpose for life here on earth—and for life everlasting—your steps will be sure.

GUARD YOUR HEART BY DIRECTING YOUR THOUGHTS

*Those who are pure in their thinking are happy,
because they will be with God.*

Matthew 5:8 NCV

How will you direct your thoughts today? Will you be an upbeat believer? Will you be a person whose hopes and dreams are alive and well? Will you put a smile on your face and a song in your heart? Hopefully so. But here's a word of warning: sometimes, when pessimism, anger, or doubt threaten to hijack your emotions, you won't feel much like celebrating. That's why you must always strive to keep your thoughts headed in the right direction.

Your thoughts have the power to lift you up or to drag you down; they have the power to energize you or deplete you, to inspire you to greater accomplishments or to make those accomplishments impossible.

What kind of attitude will you select today? Will you guard your heart by dwelling upon those things that are true, honorable, and worthy of praise? Or will you allow yourself to be swayed by the negativity that seems to dominate our troubled world?

God intends that you experience joy and abundance, but He will not force His joy upon you; you must claim it for yourself. It's up to you to celebrate the life that God has given you. So today, spend more time thinking about your blessings and less time fretting about your hardships. Then, take time to thank the Giver of all things good for gifts that are, in truth, far too numerous to count.

So prepare your minds for service and have self-control.

1 Peter 1:13 NCV

A TIP FOR GUARDING YOUR HEART

Good thoughts create good deeds. Good thoughts lead to good deeds and bad thoughts lead elsewhere. So guard your thoughts accordingly.

WORDS OF WISDOM

As we have by faith said no to sin, so we should by faith say yes to God and set our minds on things above, where Christ is seated in the heavenlies.

Vonette Bright

No more imperfect thoughts. No more sad memories. No more ignorance. My redeemed body will have a redeemed mind. Grant me a foretaste of that perfect mind as you mirror your thoughts in me today.

Joni Eareckson Tada

Believe that your tender, loving thoughts and wishes for good have the power to help the struggling souls of the earth rise higher.

Ella Wheeler Wilcox

The things we think are the things that feed our souls. If we think on pure and lovely things, we shall grow pure and lovely like them; and the converse is equally true.

Hannah Whitall Smith

Preoccupy my thoughts with your praise beginning today.

Joni Eareckson Tada

GOD'S WORDS OF WISDOM

Come near to God, and God will come near to you. You sinners, clean sin out of your lives. You who are trying to follow God and the world at the same time, make your thinking pure.

James 4:8 NCV

And now, dear brothers and sisters, let me say one more thing as I close this letter. Fix your thoughts on what is true and honorable and right. Think about things that are pure and lovely and admirable. Think about things that are excellent and worthy of praise.

Philippians 4:8 NLT

Dear friend, guard Clear Thinking and Common Sense with your life; don't for a minute lose sight of them. They'll keep your soul alive and well, they'll keep you fit and attractive.

Proverbs 3:21-22 MSG

SUMMING IT UP

Unless you're willing to guard your thoughts, you'll never be able to guard your heart.

GUARD YOUR HEART AGAINST WORRY

Don't worry about anything, but in everything,
through prayer and petition with thanksgiving,
let your requests be made known to God.

Philippians 4:6 Holman CSB

Because we are imperfect human beings struggling with imperfect circumstances, we worry. Even though we, as Christians, have the assurance of salvation—even though we, as Christians, have the promise of God's love and protection—we find ourselves fretting over the inevitable frustrations of everyday life. Jesus understood our concerns when He spoke the reassuring words found in the 6th chapter of Matthew.

Where is the best place to take your worries? Take them to God. Take your troubles to Him; take your fears to Him; take your doubts to Him; take your weaknesses to Him; take your sorrows to Him . . . and leave them all there. Seek protection from the One who offers you eternal salvation; build your spiritual house upon the Rock that cannot be moved.

Perhaps you are concerned about your future, your health, or your finances. Or perhaps you are simply a "worrier" by nature. If so, make Matthew 6 a regular part of your daily Bible reading. This beautiful passage will remind you that God still sits in His heaven and you are His beloved child. Then, perhaps, you will worry a little less and trust God a little more, and that's as it should be because God is trustworthy . . . and you are protected.

A Tip for Guarding Your Heart

An important part of becoming a more mature Christian is learning to worry less and to trust God more. And while you're at it, remember that worry is never a valid substitute for work. So do your best, and then turn your worries over to God.

WORDS OF WISDOM

Worry is the senseless process of cluttering up tomorrow's opportunities with leftover problems from today.

Barbara Johnson

Build a little fence of trust around today; fill each space with loving work and therein stay.

Mary Frances Butts

We are not called to be burden-bearers, but cross-bearers and light-bearers. We must cast our burdens on the Lord.

Corrie ten Boom

This life of faith, then, consists in just this—being a child in the Father's house. Let the ways of childish confidence and freedom from care, which so please you and win your heart when you observe your own little ones, teach you what you should be in your attitude toward God.

Hannah Whitall Smith

Today is mine. Tomorrow is none of my business. If I peer anxiously into the fog of the future, I will strain my spiritual eyes so that I will not see clearly what is required of me now.

Elisabeth Elliott

GOD'S WORDS OF WISDOM

So do not worry, saying, "What shall we eat?" or "What shall we drink?" or "What shall we wear?" For the pagans run after all these things, and your heavenly Father knows that you need them. But seek first his kingdom and his righteousness, and all these things will be given to you as well. Therefore do not worry about tomorrow, for tomorrow will worry about itself. Each day has enough trouble of its own.

Matthew 6:31-34 NIV

Come to Me, all you who labor and are heavy laden, and I will give you rest. Take My yoke upon you and learn from Me, for I am gentle and lowly in heart, and you will find rest for your souls. For My yoke is easy and My burden is light.

Matthew 11:28-30 NKJV

Jesus said, "Don't let your hearts be troubled. Trust in God, and trust in me."

John 14:1 NCV

SUMMING IT UP

You have worries, but God has solutions. Your challenge is to trust Him to solve the problems that you can't.

GUARD YOUR HEART AGAINST PERFECTIONISM

Blessed are those who do not condemn themselves.

Romans 14:22 NLT

Expectations, expectations, expectations! As a woman living in the 21st century, you know that demands can be high, and expectations even higher. The media delivers an endless stream of messages that tell you how to look, how to behave, how to eat, and how to dress. The media's expectations are impossible to meet—God's are not. God doesn't expect you to be perfect . . . and neither should you.

Remember: the expectations that really matter are God's expectations. Everything else takes a back seat. So do your best to please God, and don't worry too much about what other people think. And, when it comes to meeting the unrealistic expectations of a world gone nuts, forget about trying to be perfect—it's impossible.

When God made you, He equipped you with an array of talents and abilities that are uniquely yours. It's up to you to discover those talents and to use them, but sometimes your own perfectionism may get in the way.

If you're your own worst critic, give it up. After all, God doesn't expect you to be perfect, and if that's okay with Him, then it should be okay with you, too.

The fear of human opinion disables; trusting in God protects you from that.

Proverbs 29:25 MSG

A TIP FOR GUARDING YOUR HEART

Accept your own imperfections: If you're caught up in the modern-day push toward perfection, grow up . . . and then lighten up on yourself.

WORDS OF WISDOM

God is so inconceivably good. He's not looking for perfection. He already saw it in Christ. He's looking for affection.

Beth Moore

Excellence is not perfection, but essentially a desire to be strong in the Lord and for the Lord.

Cynthia Heald

A perfectionist resists the truth that growing up in Christ is a process.

Susan Lenzkes

God is not hard to please. He does not expect us to be absolutely perfect. He just expects us to keep moving toward Him and believing in Him, letting Him work with us to bring us into conformity to His will and ways.

Joyce Meyer

Face your deficiencies and acknowledge them; but do not let them master you. Let them teach you patience, sweetness, insight. When we do the best we can, we never know what miracle is wrought in our life, or in the life of another.

Helen Keller

GOD'S WORDS OF WISDOM

*Those who wait for perfect weather will never plant seeds;
those who look at every cloud will never harvest crops. Plant
early in the morning, and work until evening, because you
don't know if this or that will succeed. They might both do well.*

Ecclesiastes 11:4,6 NCV

*In thee, O Lord, do I put my trust; let me never be put into
confusion.*

Psalm 71:1 KJV

Teach me Your way, O Lord; I will walk in Your truth.

Psalm 86:11 NASB

*Whatever you do, work at it with all your heart, as working for
the Lord, not for men.*

Colossians 3:23 NIV

SUMMING IT UP

Don't worry about being perfect—it's impossible. God
doesn't want your perfection; He wants your heart.

GUARD YOUR HEART BY PUTTING GOD FIRST

You shall have no other gods before Me.

Exodus 20:3 NKJV

I s God your top priority? Have you given His Son your heart, your soul, your talents, and your time? Or are you in the habit of giving God little more than a few hours on Sunday morning? The answer to these questions will determine how you prioritize your days and your life.

As you contemplate your own relationship with God, remember this: All of mankind is engaged in the practice of worship. Some people choose to worship God and, as a result, reap the joy that He intends for His children. Others distance themselves from God by worshiping such things as earthly possessions or personal gratification . . . and when they do so, they suffer.

In the book of Exodus, God warns that we should place no gods before Him. Yet all too often, we place our

Lord in second, third, or fourth place as we worship the gods of pride, greed, power, or lust.

When we place our desires for material possessions above our love for God—or when we yield to temptations of the flesh—we find ourselves engaged in a struggle that is similar to the one Jesus faced when He was tempted by Satan. In the wilderness, Satan offered Jesus earthly power and unimaginable riches, but Jesus turned Satan away and chose instead to worship God. We must do likewise by putting God first and worshiping only Him.

Does God rule your heart? Make certain that the honest answer to this question is a resounding yes. In the life of every righteous believer, God comes first. And that's precisely the place that He deserves in your heart, too.

A Tip for Guarding Your Heart

Think about your priorities. Are you really putting God first in your life, or are you putting other things— things like possessions, pleasures, or personal status— ahead of your relationship with the Father. And if your priorities for life are misaligned, think of at least three things you can do today to put God where He belongs: in first place.

WORDS OF WISDOM

We shouldn't work towards being saints, but to please God.

St. Thérèse of Lisieux

If you are receiving your affirmation, love, self worth, joy, strength and acceptance from anywhere but God, He will shake it.

Lisa Bevere

Make God's will the focus of your life day by day. If you seek to please Him and Him alone, you'll find yourself satisfied with life.

Kay Arthur

Don't be addicted to approval. Follow your heart. Do what you believe God is telling you to do, and stand firm in Him and Him alone.

Joyce Meyer

If you really want to please God and intend to be in full agreement with His will, you can't go wrong.

Francis Mary Paul Libermann

GOD'S WORDS OF WISDOM

No one has seen God, ever. But if we love one another, God dwells deeply within us, and his love becomes complete in us—perfect love! This is how we know we're living steadily and deeply in him, and he in us: He's given us life from his life, from his very own Spirit.

1 John 4:12-13 MSG

He that loveth not, knoweth not God; for God is love.

1 John 4:8 KJV

Yet, O Lord, you are our Father. We are the clay, you are the potter; we are all the work of your hand.

Isaiah 64:8 NIV

God is spirit, and those who worship him must worship in spirit and truth.

John 4:24 NCV

SUMMING IT UP

You must guard your heart by putting God in His rightful place—first place.

ABOVE ALL ELSE: YOUR RELATIONSHIP WITH CHRIST

*I assure you, anyone who believes in me
already has eternal life.*

John 6:47 NLT

Eternal life is not an event that begins when you die. Eternal life begins when you invite Jesus into your heart right here on earth. So it's important to remember that God's plans for you are not limited to the ups and downs of everyday life. If you've allowed Jesus to reign over your heart, you've already begun your eternal journey.

As mere mortals, our vision for the future, like our lives here on earth, is limited. God's vision is not burdened by such limitations: His plans extend throughout all eternity.

Let us praise the Creator for His priceless gift, and let us share the Good News with all who cross our paths.

We return our Father's love by accepting His grace and by sharing His message and His love. When we do, we are blessed here on earth and throughout all eternity.

> *For God so loved the world*
> *that he gave his only Son,*
> *so that everyone who believes in him*
> *will not perish but have eternal life.*
>
> John 3:16 NLT

A TIP FOR GUARDING YOUR HEART

Your eternity with God is secure because of your belief in Jesus.

WORDS OF WISDOM

Your choice to either receive or reject the Lord Jesus Christ will determine where you spend eternity.

Anne Graham Lotz

I can still hardly believe it. I, with shriveled, bent fingers, atrophied muscles, gnarled knees, and no feeling from the shoulders down, will one day have a new body—light, bright and clothed in righteousness—powerful and dazzling.

Joni Eareckson Tada

God has promised us abundance, peace, and eternal life. These treasures are ours for the asking; all we must do is claim them. One of the great mysteries of life is why on earth do so many of us wait so very long to lay claim to God's gifts?

Marie T. Freeman

Like a shadow declining swiftly . . . away . . . like the dew of the morning gone with the heat of the day; like the wind in the treetops, like a wave of the sea, so are our lives on earth when seen in light of eternity.

Ruth Bell Graham

GOD'S WORDS OF WISDOM

*And this is the testimony: that God has given us eternal life,
and this life is in His Son. He who has the Son has life; he who
does not have the Son of God does not have life.*

1 John 5:11-12 NKJV

*Don't be troubled. You trust God, now trust in me. There are
many rooms in my Father's home, and I am going to prepare
a place for you. If this were not so, I would tell you plainly.
When everything is ready, I will come and get you, so that you
will always be with me where I am.*

John 14:1-3 NLT

*Pursue righteousness, godliness, faith, love, endurance, and
gentleness. Fight the good fight for the faith; take hold of eternal
life, to which you were called and have made a good confession
before many witnesses.*

1 Timothy 6:11-12 Holman CSB

SUMMING IT UP

God offers you a priceless gift: the gift of eternal life. If
you have not already done so, accept God's gift today—
tomorrow may be too late.

Tim Way has been on staff with Family Christian Stores for the past twenty-three years. He is currently the Senior Buyer of Book, Bibles, and Church Resources. Tim and his wife, Ramona, live in Grand Rapids, Michigan. They have three grown children and three grandchildren.

Dr. Criswell Freeman is a best-selling author with over 14,000,000 books in print. He is a graduate of Vanderbilt University. He received his doctoral degree from the Adler School of Professional Psychology in Chicago; he also attended classes at Southern Seminary in Louisville where he was mentored by the late Wayne Oates, a pioneer in the field of pastoral counseling. Dr. Freeman is married; he has two children.